THE CILANTRO DIARIES

THE CILANTRO DIARIES

BUSINESS LESSONS FROM THE MOST UNLIKELY PLACES

LORENZO GOMEZ III

LIONCREST
PUBLISHING

THE CILANTRO DIARIES

Business Lessons From the Most Unlikely Places

ISBN   978-1-61961-765-0 *Paperback*
       978-1-61961-766-7 *Ebook*

To Chuquiri and Pollo. Thank you for the gift of story.

CONTENTS

FOREWORD

BY ROBERT RIVARD

———

Lorenzo Gomez is a natural born storyteller, and it's not something he learned in school. In fact, the beauty of Lorenzo Gomez and his first book, *The Cilantro Diaries*, is that he is so self-schooled. Well, not entirely "self." It's immediately evident that what Lorenzo's family lacked in the way of material comforts was rendered all but irrelevant by the bedrock values his parents passed down to him and his siblings. Lorenzo is the product of a working-class family, and he could very well have followed in his family's trade legacy.

Fate guided Lorenzo in a different, uncharted direction. Luck plays a part in his story, as it does in anyone who enjoys success. The young man who started out stocking groceries and then sold Gateway computers soon found himself selling services at Rackspace, the world's largest managed cloud company. For the first time, he was paid a salary rather than a low hourly wage. From there, he vaulted into his present world of startups, entrepreneurship, and an innovative coworking tech space called Geekdom.

While the book focuses on lessons learned in the marketplace, it relies just as much on what Pops, Lorenzo's father, imparted in the way of timeless life lessons. What Lorenzo did not learn at home was how to succeed as a business professional, but he instinctively knew to stick to his core values. Sales? Spreadsheets? Monthly targets and quotas? Customer retention plans? Cold calling prospective clients? He simply watched the people he trusted and made them mentors. They, in turn, recognized a gem in the rough and gave their young, talented recruit the tools to succeed.

Still, Lorenzo remains a stranger in a strange land, an adaptive guy who makes adjustments and manages to thrive in every new territory in which he ventures. That's what makes *The Cilantro Diaries* such a fascinating read. Lorenzo Gomez doesn't see things the same way the average, middle-class, tech-savvy worker sees things.

Before winning his employee ID at Rackspace, Lorenzo had never been on a plane, crossed the border south into Mexico (home of his parents' forebears), or even left Texas. Suddenly, he found himself on a business trip to London.

You'll have to read past this foreword to learn how Lorenzo fared as he traveled abroad for the first time and walked into a new world, metaphorically. What is evident about Lorenzo is this: home or abroad, what he has in spades is self-esteem, street smarts, a blue-collar work ethic, and loyalty to his bosses and mentors. It is clear Lorenzo believes in himself at a gut level.

The Cilantro Diaries is a road map written for the young men and women who are motivated but not particularly strong map readers, bright but not necessarily college educated. It is a guidebook on life's road, where nothing is certain, opportunity and challenge both lie around the next curve, and how you navigate will determine the outcome of your journey more than any other factor.

I've known Lorenzo for a number of years now, and would describe him as a friend and trusted collaborator rather than a professional colleague, which doesn't capture the energy between us, or the energy Lorenzo imparts everywhere he goes and with everything he does. Read this book, and you'll fall right into that energy field and emerge on the other side feeling stronger about your own plan of action.

—ROBERT RIVARD

INTRODUCTION

"LESSONS FROM THE POLLO" OR
THINGS MY FATHER TAUGHT ME

---

*"Everyone wants to be a valued member of a
winning team on an inspiring mission."*

—FRED REICHHELD AND GRAHAM WESTON

If you ever live in San Antonio and then move away, inevitably, you'll tell people that you miss one thing about the city. It's not the Alamo, the Riverwalk, or even the mighty San Antonio Spurs.

No, you will tell people you miss your local neighborhood H-E-B grocery store. H-E-B is everyone's local supermarket, which just happens to be the largest privately held grocery chain in the United States.

In San Antonio, where I grew up and where H-E-B is head-quartered, it has always been one of the dominant companies. A true powerhouse for as long as I can remember, and my family, the Gomezes, have a long, proud legacy of working there. Five of my six siblings worked at H-E-B at one point in their lives; specifically, we worked at the store closest to our house, H-E-B Number Five.

My sisters never liked Number Five. We lived in what you might call "the hood," so they preferred shopping at one of the nicer stores like H-E-B Number Eight. H-E-B Number Five was the kind of place you could buy a Pancho Villa prayer candle, while H-E-B Number Eight had an olive bar, if you catch my drift. H-E-B Number Five may not have been the best grocery store in the world, but it was *our* store, and this is really where my story begins.

I started at H-E-B as a bagger; then they promoted me to cashier, and finally, to the produce department. The last promotion is important, because it's when they let a seventeen-year-old operate a power jack and trash com-pactor—big time stuff. Working at H-E-B was the second job I held in my life, but it was the first time I felt like I belonged somewhere.

To this day, I'm convinced I had more fun working in a produce department than anyone's ever had in the history of the world. My coworkers and I operated like a little Navy

Seal team. We'd come in, work like animals, have fun, and absolutely dominate the greens. I also learned a lot working there—lessons I've carried with me throughout the rest of my career. Many stories from my H-E-B days were memorable, but one stands out that had a major influence on me.

I'm the sixth of seven children in my family, and my mom cooked for us almost every night, so she did a *lot* of grocery shopping. Most days, she shopped at the store where I worked. Funny enough, on this particular night, I wasn't even at the store—I was at home, sitting at our kitchen table doing homework. My mom had gone to the store that night, and when she came home, she was really excited about something.

As I helped her unload groceries, she told me, "Oh, Mijo, I was in Number Five today, and as I was going through your department, I saw it on the wall above the cilantro! I saw your picture!"

I'd completely forgotten that the managers had taken photos of every employee and hung our pictures above our departments so customers could ask us for help by name. Then my mom told me, "I'm so proud of you, Mijo."

Immediately, I felt both embarrassed and annoyed, but I was a polite kid. I gave my mom a half smile and mumbled, "Oh, thanks, Mom. That's cool."

I didn't mean it though. In truth, her words triggered a reaction in me, and I remember thinking: *This is the worst thing ever.* There was no way that having my picture above the cilantro at H-E-B Number Five on West Avenue and Hildebrand was going to be the pinnacle of my career!

At the time, I felt a lot of guilt and shame over my reaction, because there's nothing wrong with working at a grocery store. Most of my siblings had been employed by H-E-B and prided themselves on working hard—it was tradition. I didn't have a problem with my coworkers, either. I loved everybody I worked with at the store, and the company treated their employees and customers great. But I realized there was something pent up in my gut that wanted more.

I thought about my photo hanging above the bright green cilantro display and told myself, "I am not going out like that." It may have only been a change in attitude, but that choice changed the course of my life. That day, I made a secret vow that if I wanted my picture on the wall, I was going to do something worthy of having it up there.

THAT WAS THEN, THIS IS NOW

About two decades later, when I had several years of experience in tech under my belt, I found myself struggling with a crisis of confidence and serious imposter syndrome. I had a new, well-paying job, but my roots were still in my neighborhood near H-E-B Number Five. There was a disconnect between where I'd come from and where I was now—my upbringing in the hood had affected my mindset and left me questioning myself. Did I really belong in this new field? I couldn't fully articulate my feelings about my career change until I attended a startup event and heard my first founder story.

The person telling the story was the managing director of a big tech accelerator, and he described talking to a customer shortly after starting his first company. He said, "The whole time I was talking to the customer, I felt like I was three cleverly designed questions away from being exposed as the fraud that I am. I never felt like an entrepreneur."

There I was, sitting in the audience, when a lightbulb went off. I felt like what he said was the theme of my career. I didn't think I was qualified to be doing the work I was doing. I feared I was only there because I'd lucked out. But I realized I didn't get to where I was in my career through luck, and that's what this book is about: how I figured out that you can pick up valuable skills and lessons from everyday people, everyday places, and everyday situations. I would like to translate them for you and pay forward the goodness that so many people have given me.

Few people can attribute their success to luck alone. You'll almost always see multiple factors at play that helped a person rise in their career, and many of them are rooted in choices. I started out in the retail grocery store business and was dragged kicking and screaming into the IT industry by my best friend, a decision that completely altered the trajectory of my career. I began working at Rackspace, one of the first tech companies in San Antonio. After nearly ten years, I left Rackspace to join another startup, CityVoice. Shortly after, that startup failed.

Then, through a series of life-changing events that I'll describe later, I began working for a man named Graham Weston. I founded the 80/20 Foundation, Graham's philanthropic arm, which grants money to San Antonio–based nonprofits, and helped invest millions of dollars into the San Antonio community. A few years later, I expanded my career again and got involved with the local startup scene. Today, I'm the executive director of the 80/20 Foundation; the CEO of one of the largest coworking spaces in Texas, Geekdom; the cofounder of the tech advocacy group, Tech Bloc; and the director of BrandTeamSix.

CAREER TIMELINE

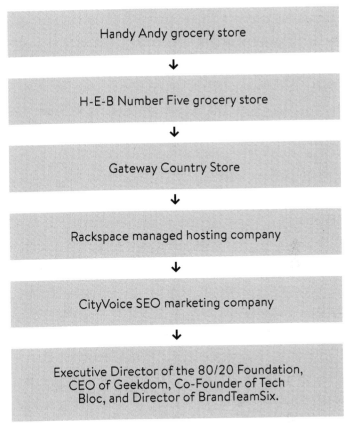

Handy Andy grocery store

↓

H-E-B Number Five grocery store

↓

Gateway Country Store

↓

Rackspace managed hosting company

↓

CityVoice SEO marketing company

↓

Executive Director of the 80/20 Foundation, CEO of Geekdom, Co-Founder of Tech Bloc, and Director of BrandTeamSix.

If you had told me growing up that I would go from bagging groceries to helping a local business legend run two of his companies, I would have told you to stop eating stupid sandwiches. That's what happened though, and the funny part is, on paper, I have no credentials that would inherently qualify me for those roles. It wasn't a college degree or specialized training that got me in the door, but it was the result of the principles I'm going to explain in this book, principles that I picked up from everyday people and places around me. Anyone with the willingness to listen, learn, and do, can apply these principles in their own lives to create the conditions for improving themselves.

However, the principles you can use to succeed aren't as simple as following a checklist. Checklists are for completing tasks—these principles are more complex, but also more effective. They're a journey. You could spend years searching for them, and it would be a career well spent, but I hope to save you some pain. It's my goal to share the lessons I've learned from the people in my life and pay their help and guidance forward so that you can spend less time searching for principles that work and more time applying them in your own life.

THE GREATEST PIECE OF BUSINESS ADVICE

A few years before I wrote this book, Graham Weston and I worked with a nonprofit called Venture for America (VFA). It's an organization similar in concept to Teach for America, but with a focus on helping young entrepreneurs. As part of the VFA fellowship, a young woman named Emily Bowe from Venture for America, Graham, and I went to Texas A&M University to assist them in launching a sales program being funded by the 80/20 Foundation.

During our visit, a legendary professor named Dr. Kerry Litzenberg did a question-and-answer session with Graham.

They spoke in front of two classes with about one hundred students from the agricultural economics program. During the Q&A, one student asked Graham, "What is the greatest piece of business advice you've learned?"

Graham gave a fantastic answer. He said, "The greatest thing I've learned in my career is that everyone wants to be a valued member of a winning team on an inspiring mission." That one sentence is worthy of a whole book, and we'll touch on it in a later chapter, but at the time, I realized I didn't know what I would have said if I were in Graham's shoes.

While he spoke on stage, I sat in the back of the auditorium and had a moment of personal panic. I wondered, if someone asked me the same question, what would my answer be? What advice would I give a student or my nieces and nephews about entering the workforce? I put a lot of thought into how to respond to that question, and this book is my answer.

This book contains principles I learned from my father and Graham, as well as others I learned throughout my career. All of these principles were handed down to me from older, wiser, cooler, and everything-er people than me, and that's how I know they're awesome—because they didn't come from me. These ideas are little treasures that are worth holding up to the sun and passing along to the people who are important to you. Looking back on my journey, I am so humbled by the sheer number of people who took the time to stop, pull me aside, and explain the world to me. They took the time to invest in me and my journey. It's my turn to stop and explain to you what I've learned, because it was so valuable to me.

THE PRINCIPLES OF POPS

My extended family has a nickname for my father—Pollo. It means chicken in Spanish, and he earned this nickname because, when he was little, he'd follow my grandmother around everywhere she went like a little baby chick. My relatives still call him Pollo to this day, but my siblings and I have always called our father Pops.

Much of what I've learned, I learned from my parents. My father always had useful Pop-isms to offer—pithy little phrases filled with wisdom—which have been tested and proven over the years. To provide some background, I grew up in a very religious household as the sixth of seven kids. My parents went through so much trial and error while raising my siblings that by the time they got to me, they had mastered many of these principles the hard way.

A usually stern and stoic man, Pops made it known that he wasn't our friend, but our father; it was his job to guide us through life. While he didn't always say much, what he did say was serious. I'll briefly explain his set of principles and dive deeper into the ones I think you will benefit from alongside other principles I've added over the years.

THE NINE FUNDAMENTAL LIFE
PRINCIPLES OF POPS

I. Keep Jesus in your heart.

I grew up in a devout Christian household, so "Keep Jesus in your heart" was my parents' number-one principle. Even into our thirties and forties, if anyone in my family dated someone, the first question my parents asked was always, "Do they love Jesus?"

An unexpected result of this principle is that it helped me learn how to set expectations with other people. Growing up, I would always warn friends before they came to my house that the price of admission was a small sermon from my parents. They'd bust out a double barrel of Jesus on anybody who walked through their door. My parents didn't expect all our guests to agree with them, but it was their right to talk about it.

II. Marry a girl who will live with you in a cardboard box.

My father used to give me this advice on romantic relationships, but I'd always wonder how to screen for it on a date. You can expect to get some strange looks if you ask, "Excuse me, I know that we've just met, but what are your feelings on being so in love with someone that you would live with them in a cardboard box? This is one of my criteria per my father." When I was older, I realized what my dad meant—associate with people who will stay loyal to you, even at your lowest point.

III. Nothing good happens after midnight.

My family would often watch the news during dinner, and my father would stop eating and repeat this phrase every time an incident took place late at night. Local robbery at 2:00 a.m.? Shaking his head, he'd then say, "Nothing good happens after midnight." Arsonist at four in the morning? "See, Lencho? Nothing good happens after midnight."

IV. If drugs and alcohol were good for you, I would have been the first to show them to you.

One of my vices growing up was smoking cigarettes, and I heard this principle from my dad every time smoking came up in a conversation. He'd get so mad, but he would tell me that he had my best interests at heart.

V. There's nothing worse than a kid with no manners.

My dad would use this phrase whenever we were in public and saw a kid acting out. It was his way of saying, "If you want to be esteemed in my world, you will have manners." It was a very persuasive way to get me and my siblings to behave, because what kid doesn't want love and affirmation from their father? Over the years, good manners have become a sort of superpower that I have in my back pocket.

VI. Dance with the one who brought you.

This principle is all about loyalty and not forgetting about the people who helped you get to where you are. It's also about sticking with things that work. If you have a tried-and-true way of accomplishing your goals, don't abandon that approach.

VII. The only thing you can control is your attitude.

My dad would say this whenever I came home from work feeling defeated by a difficult customer. His point was, essentially, don't let them get to you. It's so easy to let people affect you, but you can choose how to react. Deciding to have a good attitude is empowering, because it takes away the control other people think they have over you.

VIII. If in doubt, there is no doubt.

This is a principle my dad used to say all the time, and I never understood what it meant until I was older. At its simplest level, it means trust your gut. If you're not sure whether something is the right choice, it probably isn't.

IX. Who you choose as your friends matters.

Perhaps more than any other principle, this one kept me out of trouble in my teenage years. People tend to want to spend time with those who make them feel good and share common interests, but those people may not be good for you. Your friends will contribute to your pool of ideas and profoundly affect your worldview, so choose wisely.

These nine principles were my father's gift to help me navigate life. The first four guided me the most in my adolescent years, whereas the last five have been invaluable throughout my career. They were the sticks of dynamite that blew down walls and obstacles when I needed them most. Pops's principles inspired me to compile my own list of career-focused principles. In fact, you'll notice several of his principles explored on a deeper level throughout this book, alongside other principles I picked up on my journey into the workforce.

Maybe you grew up in a situation like mine—a big family, not a lot of money, and living in the hood without a college degree. Whatever your situation, I'm here to tell you that you can achieve more than having your portrait displayed over the cilantro section in a grocery store. If you want to change your life, the lessons can be found in everyday people, places, and situations. All you have to do is notice them.

SECTION I

CREATING YOUR PERSONAL BOARD OF DIRECTORS

YOUR DEPUTIES LOVE YOU

—————

"A friend is someone who knows all about you and still loves you."

—ELBERT HUBBARD

My career in tech didn't start until I worked at a magical place called Rackspace. I was twenty years old with no college degree, no clue what the Internet was, and no idea what world I had just entered. To this day, I can't explain my job at Rackspace to my mother. At a certain point, I said to her, "Just tell everyone I work for the Internet, and let's call it a day," but what really happened is I went from selling computers at Gateway to handling customer accounts for the number one managed hosting company on the Internet—Rackspace.

Getting that job at Rackspace changed my life. Prior to working there, I had never been on an airplane. I had visited the Laredo side of the Mexican border, but never left the state of Texas. After I got my job at Rackspace, my brother took me to Vegas. Then, Rackspace put me on the second flight of my life, which was to one of the busiest airports in the world—Heathrow in London.

I suddenly found myself in new situations, dealing with new problems, and meeting new people—people who were working professionals, including some of the most intelligent people I've met in my life. Three individuals have had an enormous influence on my career and have introduced me to the idea of a personal board of directors.

Graham Weston was the chairman and first investor of Rackspace. The company's first CEO was Lanham Napier, and Lew Moorman was the president. These were the guys who scaled Rackspace up to be a publicly traded company, and they had a cool practice they used called "the Open Book." Every month, they would gather the whole company together and walk us through the company's financials— how much we spent, how much revenue we pulled in, how many customers we lost, and so on.

Prior to my time at Rackspace, I had never been treated like a true professional. As you can imagine, I was awestruck by the level of transparency we were given at the Open

Books, and it was a gesture that solidified my loyalty to the company. Even more so, I felt honored that these smart guys—professionals who had graduated from Texas A&M, Harvard Business School, and Stanford Law—trusted my coworkers and me with such heavy information. Then one day, Graham, Lanham, and Lew talked about the Rackspace Board of Directors.

They spoke about the board with such reverence that I had to pull someone aside and have them explain to me what exactly a board of directors did. When I heard, I thought it was the craziest thing in the world. These three men, whom I already thought were the smartest guys on Earth, reported to men and women who were possibly even smarter? The bosses had bosses of their own? Insanity.

This revelation felt like unlocking a bonus level of a video game or discovering a mythical Jedi council. I imagined a room full of wise, bearded men dropping bombs of wisdom, and it made me realize something: everyone, even the smartest people, need advice from others. In the case of a company like Rackspace, those others are the board of directors. It's the board's job to make sure the company is moving in a copacetic direction and that its mission is executed. They want the company to succeed.

PERSONAL BOARD OF DIRECTORS, ASSEMBLE!

Why should the concept of a board of directors matter to you as a young professional? Because, in the same way a successful company has a board of directors looking out for its best interests, you can have a personal board of directors looking out for you.

It took a couple years after learning about company boards for me to realize that there are a handful of people in my life who are always there to help when I get into a jam. They tell me truths that no one else is willing to tell me and give me advice that no one else knows me well enough to give. They are my personal board of directors.

For your board of directors, think about who in your life is there to guide you. For example, maybe it's your parents. In the early stages of life, parents tend to take care of Maslow's hierarchy of needs for you—they keep you safe, give you shelter, and put food in your belly. When you're older, you can choose to keep them on your board to help with the higher tiers of needs—achieving your full potential, making career and life choices, and so on. The thing is, it's up to you who's on your board. Nobody is entitled to a spot.

The first person whom I realized was on my board of directors by choice was my brother Danny. He was the person throughout my upbringing who routinely pulled me aside and said, "Hey, man, I need to explain something to you that no one else is going to explain." The people in your life who are willing to do that for you are invaluable. Danny has always been able to approach me with that level of honesty, and it's one reason I now consider him to be the chairman of my board.

WHY A PERSONAL BOARD OF DIRECTORS IS IMPORTANT

You might wonder, "Why have an entire board? I have my spouse/best friend/parent for support." First and foremost, you want multiple people on your board because no *one* person can fill all the roles you need in your life. Also, you need diversity on your board—everyone can't have the same perspective as you.

Diversity has become a clichéd term with everyone saying that we need it, but few people explaining why. Personally, the why came to life for me when my job at Rackspace relocated me from Texas to London. In my first two weeks in London, I was completely blown away by all the people I met who had traveled to London from all over the world. Growing up in the inner city of San Antonio, I'd only ever met Hispanics and Anglos—I'd never met anyone with a foreign accent.

One of the first things I noticed was that everybody had a different worldview. The world is so rich with diversity, and different people can bring different perspectives to the table. They can give you ideas that may have never occurred to you on your own, ideas that may be better than yours. I talked with people who were from places like dictator-led, war-torn countries, and they shared perspectives that my own experiences could never produce.

Now, the people on your board of directors don't have to be from a radically different background than you. They can be the same age as you with more experience in a given area or be someone who has different interests than you. The point is that there has to be some form of differentiation, because it's the times when different ideas collide that will teach you the most.

Second, you want a board of directors because humans at a primal level are communal beings. We crave community. Nothing has brought this to life for me more than running a technology coworking space. In my opinion, there's no greater *lonely* than big-city lonely, when you're surrounded by millions of people but don't know any of them. Don't let that happen to you. If you're able to find or create your own community in the form of a board of directors, it can be the most important support structure you have in your life.

Third, you need people to help you break down data. Your board of directors is there to tell you when you're misreading information or looking at a situation the wrong way.

Sometimes, you want data to say one thing, and it becomes impossible to see it differently. When that happens, you need another set of unbiased eyes to look at the situation and set you straight.

For example, one day I walked into the office and heard a young college graduate who worked for me at the time trying to solve a problem with our teammates. It quickly became obvious that she didn't have a work problem; her predicament was over a boy. She'd been to a barbeque the previous weekend, and much flirting and laughing had transpired between her and the subject in question.

Naturally, she followed up with said boy, but alas, her e-mails and texts elicited no response. She grew more frustrated and angry trying to solve the mystery. What happened? What changed? He seemed so friendly and everything had gone so well.

So, I asked her a question: "Were you both drinking?"

"Yes."

"*There* is your problem."

The human brain is constantly trying to break down data in all situations. When a person who catches your eye is involved, it tends to work even harder. The problem in her scenario was alcohol. Nothing against it, but drinking has a way of screwing up data. An accidental brush of the shoulder when sober has a completely different meaning than a brush of the shoulder when drinking.

I told her, "Because you were both drinking, your data is contaminated."

I think I helped her resolve her anxiety over the issue because she died laughing and wrote "contaminated data" on the whiteboard next to us, and then went on with her day.

My point is that when you're misreading a situation, a good board member helps you break down the data.

WHAT KIND OF PEOPLE MAKE THE BEST BOARD MEMBERS?

In general, you want to surround yourself with people who have your best interests at heart—this goes double for your board members. Don't put someone on your board if you can't trust them not to screw you over! That defeats the whole point, because your board is there to give you opinions that you value and can trust. Instead, choose the people who, even if they had to share bad news or tell you something you didn't want to hear, you would never doubt them, because you know they love you unconditionally; choose someone who would congratulate you if you painted the world's most beautiful painting rather than someone who would be jealous.

You also want to choose people who accept who you are as a person. If you're quirky and like to bust out into spontaneous song while you're walking down the street, your board members should appreciate that about you. They're not people who are trying to get you to change. It's good if they want what's best for you, but what they think is best for you should mesh with your worldview. Respect between you and your board members needs to go both ways.

Keep in mind, you need the social-emotional support of your board members as much as you need their expertise. Until you can plug a syringe into the back of your head Matrix-style, you can't do it all by yourself, so stop stressing about it. If you stop trying to solve all your problems on your own and instead start looking for people who can supplement you as your board members, you'll be much more successful.

WHEN THE PICKINGS ARE SLIM

There are many great benefits to having a diverse group of individuals on your personal board of directors, but having an abundance of supportive people in your life isn't always possible. Maybe you're from a rough neighborhood, you grew up as an only child, your parents split when you were young, or you moved to another country where everyone is a stranger. You need to know that even having one board member is enough. It's not ideal, but it's fine, and much better than having no board members at all. If you find that you don't even have one person you can trust to give you guidance, I want this book to be your board member. Think of me like a big brother giving you advice, and start from there.

You can go your whole life with only one board member—one best friend who won't let you fall into ruin—but I predict that as you advance in your career, you'll meet many more people who you can invite to join your board of directors. In the meantime, you might be thinking, "How can I amass this Jedi council? I don't know many people who are wise, educated, or successful."

I'm here to tell you, it's okay. There's no rush, so don't feel bad about starting with only one. Growing up, my only board member was my brother Danny. Then in high school, I added my friend Dax. At the start of my career, I added only one or two other board members, and it wasn't until later that I met more people I could trust. Nobody starts with a whole army of people, so don't lose hope. Just one good board member can help you make better decisions and avoid a whole lot of heartache throughout your life.

CHOOSING YOUR BOARD MEMBERS

One of the most beautiful things about a personal board of directors is that **the only people on it are the ones you deputize**. For the first time in your life, you can be the king or queen who gets to knight someone, or the sheriff who deputizes people to help them keep order.

You might have some candidates in mind, but what if someone doesn't meet your standards? Simple—you don't give them the honor. Nobody is owed a place on your board. However, when you *do* choose someone to be on your board, it's important for you to let them know.

You have to tell them, "I've deputized you to be on my board, which means:

- I value your ideas.
- I want to discuss decisions with you.
- I want you to help me break down the hard questions in life.
- I want you to push back on me when I'm wrong.
- I want you to fight with me when it matters.
- I want you to tell me when I'm lying to myself.
- I want you to tell me when I'm full of bullshit.
- You're in the category of friends who can tell me things that other people can't."

People want to know you've chosen them, that you think they're special, and that you value their opinion over others'.

It's a gift you can give to the people who are important to you—a gift that should be guarded with great care.

Deputizing someone to your board is a decision that deserves special consideration, in part because being your board member, or deputy, comes with a lot of responsibility. You're counting on your deputies to tell you the hard truths—the things nobody wants to talk about—and that isn't easy for them or for you.

First, here is a quick definition of a hard truth. There are normal facts and truths in the world that you can just Google and be on your way, but then there are other truths that are more complex. It's a fact that everyone wakes up in the morning, but it's a hard truth to realize that you are not a morning person. Even more to the point, a hard truth is when someone tells you that, in the morning, you are a jerk. Stings, I know.

A hard truth is something specific to you that other people see but you have trouble seeing in yourself. No one wants to tell you about hard truths, and for good reason—most of the time, they are not easy to hear. That is why I believe only board members can be the ones who deliver this kind of truth.

My best example of a hard truth has to do with one of my nephews. Growing up, he was obsessed with basketball and so knowledgeable about the sport that ESPN could have hired him to throw out stats on demand. He was actually pretty good at playing, but there was a problem. Gomez men, on average, are between five foot eight and five eleven. Most of us don't break six feet tall, and if you want to be in the NBA, height is kind of a must-have.

A hard truth would be for me to pull my nephew aside and tell him, "Look, brother, I know you love basketball and want to be in the NBA. That is a great goal, but I am here to tell you that our family is not a tall family. So, there is a very high probability that you may not make it. If you want to have a basketball career, there are lots of jobs you can do in the NBA, but being point guard for the Spurs is probably not one of them. No matter what happens, I love you, and I will be your biggest fan, on or off the court."

When your board member comes to you with a hard truth, it's your job to adhere to a philosophy that Marc Andreessen, one of the founding pioneers of the Internet, succinctly put in four words: "strong opinions loosely held." This means you should have strong, informed opinions, but be ready to abandon them when you're presented with more compelling facts. If your deputy tells you you're wrong and gives evidence to the claim, don't fight them on it. Be open to new ideas and leave your ego at the door.

It took a little time for me to adopt this philosophy myself.

Once, I worked with a guy from Forbes on a project that involved writing an article. I gave the article to him to review, and he completely chopped it up with edits. I was *so* offended, but he gave me some good, if not darkly humorous, advice. "When it comes to writing, Lorenzo, you can never be afraid to drown your kittens." He was really saying that you should never be so attached to an idea that you can't let it go. Try to think of someone reshaping your ideas as a positive—your ideas will come out stronger in the end—and don't take criticism as a personal attack.

I always admired Graham, Lanham, and Lew for their ability to argue ferociously but then quickly move to the right idea after all the facts were presented. It's a hard thing to do because people often think changing opinions is a sign of weakness, that it means you can't make up your mind and are a flip-flopper. I'm here to tell you that's wrong. If you're able to be thoughtful, use logic when presented with facts, and surrender your idea for something better, it can be the most powerful tool in your professional toolbox.

ROLES ON YOUR PERSONAL BOARD OF DIRECTORS

Every great board of directors should include people with diverse personalities and skill sets who serve different roles. You may come up with others for your own personal board, but the following roles have served me well.

THE GANDALF

What I've always loved about Gandalf in *The Lord of the Rings* is that he isn't loose with his words. He's thoughtful, wise, and doesn't talk for the sake of filling the air. For your board of directors, a person like Gandalf can be your strongest ally. In my case, the Gandalf role was filled by my father. When my father gave advice, he was really giving a gift, because he didn't have a lot of money or a college degree. But he always had wise words. His words were the greatest gift he gave and have helped me so much throughout my life.

When you're assembling your board of directors, don't overlook the quiet Gandalf character. One of the Gandalf's greatest strengths is their years of experience, a strength that many less-experienced individuals try to fake. When I was a manager at Rackspace, I'd regularly work with young professionals who confused mastering tasks with mastering their role's experiences. These employees would come to me after six months in a new position and say they'd outgrown their current role and were ready to move on.

What they really meant was that they'd mastered a task performed in that role. I'd ask them whether they had ever dealt with a fight between two customers that resulted in stolen data or had a customer who was extorted by Russian hackers. They'd say no, and I'd tell them that only time serves up those experiences. You need experiences to draw upon, which is why you need the Gandalf character. To truly master a role, you must be able to capably handle any situation it throws at you, especially situations that require you to solve interpersonal problems. Technology may change rapidly but human nature doesn't, and managing people is what the Gandalf knows better than most.

THE BATMAN

The Batman character is the person who isn't as experienced or as wise as Gandalf yet, but is close enough to you to tell you the things that are around the corner. They're the Batman to your Robin, the person who shows you the ropes and watches your back like an older brother. I know many people have older brothers who are bullies, but those aren't the type of brothers I'm talking about. I'm talking about the older brother who loves you unconditionally; keeps your deepest, darkest secrets; and goes out of his way to protect you.

As I mentioned earlier in the book, my brother Danny has always filled this role for me, and he has a saying, "It's all good, brother." It's his way of telling me, "Nothing you say is going to change how I look at you. The state of the world is okay. You can be heartbroken and depressed, but I'm here telling you that it's all good. There is stability in your life and it's standing right next to you." Find the person in your life who fills this role and put them on your board.

THE SCOOBY GANG

The Scooby Gang includes your close, trusted friends. As a group, you all have unique strengths and weaknesses, and your friends help you solve problems in your life. In my case, two of my most important board members are people I knew growing up. They are my friends Dax and Luke. Dax was the guy who would tell it like it is, and Luke was the guy who could dig deep on a particular subject.

You don't need to share all the same interests as your Scooby Gang, but it's important that you connect with them on a personal level. I actually couldn't stand Dax or Luke when I first met them, but after realizing what beautiful, smart human beings they were, I wanted them on my board.

THE SPOCK

During my time in London, I was briefly roommates with a guy named Brian Thomson, or BT. BT is smart—he has an MBA, among other accomplishments—but what stands out to me is how he never lets emotions cloud his judgment. Like Spock from *Star Trek*, BT represents the objective businessperson on my board who could take the emotion out of a situation and make an objective call. I'm the opposite, in that I have a hard time emotionally detaching from decisions. If you're the same, it's important to have an objective person like Spock on your board.

THE YODA

The next person who played a huge role on my board was my pastor, Doug Robins. This book isn't about religion, but for me, Doug represents the true, nonjudgmental friend who won't let you fall into ruin. A lot of pastors and authority figures might judge you and say that if you do something they disagree with, you'll suffer the consequences. Doug was the opposite.

In *Star Wars*, Yoda trains Luke in the swamps of Dagobah without revealing his status as one of the most powerful Jedi of all time—he doesn't lord his title or status over Luke; he just gives Luke the tools and knowledge to make the right decisions for himself. Like Yoda, Doug provided council without forcing his opinions on me and helped guide me through some of the greatest decisions of my life. Whether or not they are a religious figure, you need someone like Yoda to guide you without coercion or judgment.

THE DOCTOR

The Doctor is the person on your board who questions your motivations. I'm not talking about *Doctor Who*, but Dr. Ian Malcolm, played by Jeff Goldblum in *Jurassic Park*. In the movie, Dr. Malcolm has a line, "Your scientists were so preoccupied with whether or not they could that they didn't stop to think if they should." He's saying, slow down and ask yourself why you're doing this. Do you have a genuine thirst for scientific advancement, or do you just want to open a flashy theme park?

My Doctor is a razor-sharp South African guy I met while working in London named Pravesh Mistry. I learned from Pravesh that you should always check your motivations and figure out why you're doing what you're doing. His signature phrase is "What motivation is driving the bus?" Like anything else in life, there are good motivations and bad motivations. For example, if you're picking a study partner, are you choosing the person who will help you the most or the person you want to ask out on a date? What motivation is driving the bus? So many situations in life require you to check your motivations, and a good Doctor can give you a gut check on those things.

GIVE YOUR BOARD MEMBERS PERMISSION TO TELL YOU HARD TRUTHS

If you've chosen your board members, even if it's just a board of one, you've done a lot of the work. Now you need to know how to work with them. First, keep in mind that your board members aren't mind readers. If you want advice, you have to ask for it.

I learned this lesson from BT. Between our personalities and shared interests, BT and I always got along well. For example, he was a movie buff, and we loved all the same Wes

Anderson films. He was calm, objective, and unemotional. We rarely disagreed, but one time in particular stands out.

After I returned to San Antonio from London, BT had earned the title of managing director, which is a fancy British way of saying he was the president of the London Rackspace office, and I'd begun reporting to a team leader I didn't like. This was during the more immature days of my career, when I didn't know how to control my mouth if I disagreed with someone. On top of making a lot of noise, I had a real talent for firing up the people around me against my target. I'd incite people by saying things like, "Oh, that person's worthless," or "He's such a bureaucrat."

One day, after receiving a lot of push-back from my team leader, I called BT on the phone. He's a busy guy, so I was really happy he took the call. I said, "Man, BT, I need your advice," and started telling him about the situation, but here's the thing: I approached BT asking for his advice, but I was all worked up—desperate, angry, frustrated, and afraid—and didn't truly want his opinion. I wanted him to agree with me. I told BT all about the situation and tried to sell him on the fact that this leader was worthless and bad for the company. I'll never forget ranting into my cell phone, pacing in a circle in the parking lot as I told BT the story.

BT patiently waited for me to finish and get it all out.

Then I stopped talking, expecting him to agree with me about what a piece of trash the team leader was, but that's not what happened.

Instead, BT told me, "All right, Lorenzo. I want you to listen up, because I'm going to give you some advice."

I grinned on the other end of the phone and thought, *Oh, this is going to be great. BT is a smart guy, and he's going to say this leader's full of it.*

Then BT shocked me by saying, "I need you to cease and desist from this day forward making any politically charged statements. You need to do your job with a good attitude. Cease and desist, now and forever."

What he meant was, "Stop causing drama, dude. Get over it and move on." I was devastated. I remember inhaling deeply and grinding my teeth, then dropping my shoulders. Hearing BT disagree with me was such a crushing blow, but he was right. No matter how angry and frustrated I felt, there was no way I could fight him on it. I knew in that moment that every word he'd said was completely true.

With one swift kick in the ass, he recalibrated my view of the world and changed my attitude. Though the scolding stung, it worked because I admired and respected BT. If anyone else on the planet had told me to cease and desist, I might've punched them in the face, but I valued BT's opinion and wanted to be the kind of person he'd admire, too.

Sometimes, you need someone to call you out. Think about the people on your board. Who would tell it to you straight? Once you've identified them, tell them how it's best done to minimize the sting. For example, you might say, "Hey, call me out, but be gentle because I'm struggling right now." Or tell me, "We are about to have a board moment of hard truth." Give them permission to tell you the hard truths in a way that won't leave you destroyed.

Sometimes being called out is formal, and sometimes it's informal. BT injected some hard truths into my life informally, whereas my friend Dax formally asked me to call him out. Dax was considering leaving his job when he asked me, "Hey, bro? Would you tell me if I'm lying to myself?" He was really asking, "Am I not happy in this job, or am I a guy who won't be happy in *any* job? Is there something wrong with me?"

There wasn't anything wrong with Dax, and I gave him my honest opinion—that he eventually needed to become an entrepreneur and be his own boss. It was one of the closest moments of my friendship with Dax, because he formally asked me as a board member to speak a hard truth into his life, and that interaction made us stronger. In your life, don't be afraid to ask for the hard truths.

AVOID LEARNING THE HARD WAY

I was stubborn growing up, and there have been many times in my life when I've had to learn a lesson the hard way. Sometimes, it took a board member pushing their way in to give me advice. When I was in my twenties, my pastor, Doug, saw that I wasn't serious about a girl I was dating. One afternoon, he called me on the phone and told me that what I was doing was wrong and that I needed to break up with her. I was surprised to hear that Doug was nearly in tears as he told me how this girl didn't deserve to be hurt. I didn't have sinister intentions, but he could tell that I was going to break her heart.

I wish this was a story with a happy ending, but it's not. I was too immature to take his advice, and sure enough, I ended up breaking that girl's heart. Unintentionally hurting that girl when I could've avoided it is one of the regrets in my life; I learned my lesson the hard way. But I also learned to trust my board members when they tell me there's a problem.

I'll never forget the pain in Doug's voice that day. He wasn't angry or judgmental—he was helping me, and there's a big difference. Doug was genuinely concerned and couldn't let me continue down a road where I would hurt myself or others without saying something.

That's the most important thing a good board member does— they intervene with love.

WE DON'T SPEAK HARD TRUTHS TO PEOPLE WHOSE BOARDS WE'RE NOT ON

As a word of warning, don't be afraid to give hard truths to your board members if they ask, but do not under any circumstances insert yourself into other people's boards when you're not invited. One of the biggest sources of conflicts you can create with another person is speaking an unsolicited hard truth when they haven't deputized you for the task.

One day in the office, a young coworker came to me and said, "I'm working with a vendor who's from my hometown, and she's making herself sound foolish on our conference calls. I want to give her this feedback. Do you think that's a good idea?"

Now, knowing my coworker wasn't friends with this vendor, there was only one good answer. I told her without blinking, **"We do not speak hard truths to people whose boards we are not on**. If you tell her that, she's more than likely going to have a very bad reaction."

When you speak a hard truth to someone who does not consider you a board member, there are only negative outcomes, even if your intentions are good. At best, they'll write you off as rudely interfering in their business; at worst, they'll be violently offended by what you have to say. The only notable exception to this rule is if you are a manager; in which case, you may need to give direct and difficult feedback to a subordinate who is missing the mark and affecting your business. Aside from that specific scenario, please, for the love of all that is holy and pure, do not speak hard truths to people whose board you are not on. As the country singer Kacey Musgraves says, "Mind your own biscuits and life will be gravy."

WHO YOU HANG OUT WITH MATTERS

———

*"Tell me who your friends are, and
I will tell you who you are."*

—MOMMA GOMEZ

Influence can be either a guiding light or a powerful weapon that others wield over you if you let them. The people you spend time with will, inevitably, influence you, which is why who you hang out with matters. My father often repeated this phrase when I was growing up, urging me and my siblings to be wary of associating with bad influences. Influences aren't limited to the company you keep, either—what you read, what you listen to, and what you watch all will influence you.

My brothers and I were pretty into punk and grunge music in the nineties, and my mom always complained about it. She said we needed to stop listening to "Burt Cocaine" because he was beckoning us to "kill the cops and do the drugs." Of course, she meant Kurt Cobain, and he was not telling us to kill cops, but he did have a profound influence on my punk rock ethos. While music and media can play a significant role in forming your worldview, the biggest influence in your life will usually be your friends.

TWO KIDS ON A DEAD-END STREET

The first time I had to make a choice about who I allowed to influence me was with my next-door neighbor Isaiah. As the youngest boy out of seven children in my family, all of my brothers were at least five years older than me, which is a dramatic difference when you're a child. As the boy closest in age to me on a literal dead-end street, Isaiah was the only one to play with, so we became friends.

Unfortunately, Isaiah came from a rough family and developed a lot of problems: drug use, a tendency to get into fights, and a fierce need to stir up trouble. Nonetheless, I began to look up to him because he had street smarts, and as a physically smaller kid, I admired Isaiah's ability to hold his own in fights. Isaiah and I went to different schools, but we both lived in the same rough inner-city district, and my peers respected physical strength.

Kids at my school were always looking for a chance to tease each other, and one experience stands out in my memory that illustrates how unintimidating I was. In gym class one day, the coach had us determine our maximum bench press weights. When I stepped up to the press machine, the coach set it on the lowest level, sixty pounds, but I couldn't lift it. Normally, performing that poorly would have been followed by a wave of teasing, but all my classmates were so embarrassed for me that nobody said a word.

Often, our own insecurities affect the type of people who draw our admiration, which can be problematic. Being snubbed in gym class was a shameful experience, and Isaiah, despite being a troublesome kid, represented the qualities I wished I possessed. I didn't know how to respond to dangerous or unpredictable situations, but he always seemed to know what to do.

In one instance, Isaiah and I were walking home after playing basketball one day when a car pulled up beside us. A man got out holding a shotgun, and I quickly decided that I was going to mirror however Isaiah responded. You never realize the weight of how helpless you are until you see a guy holding a shotgun for no good reason other than to show you he is the alpha. It's one of those law-of-the-jungle moments that demonstrates how truly easy it is for the strong to overcome the weak. Isaiah knew how to handle the situation coolly, and eventually, the man got back in his car and drove away. In that situation and many others, I felt that Isaiah was a sort of armor, and I was safe with him. Around that time, I decided it was acceptable to hang out with Isaiah, even if he was a bad kid, as long as I didn't violate my personal morals.

THE POWER OF SAYING NO

For the first time in my life, I was confronted with the idea of veto power. If Isaiah wanted me to join him in an activity that would've landed us in trouble, like tagging a building or stealing a car, I would refuse. Turning down your peers is a difficult choice to make, especially when you're young, because you don't want them to reject you. For me, it was a choice between making a good decision and avoiding ridicule—fortunately, I chose to do the right thing.

I could have been negatively influenced by Isaiah; in the same way, the choice to do the right thing stemmed from the influence of others. Young adults tend to adopt their moral compass from their family, and unlike Isaiah, I was more afraid of disappointing my parents and siblings than I was of the police. I was also governed by a hefty dose of Christian guilt that compelled me to avoid trouble. While guilt kept me in line as a kid, I want to warn you that letting guilt rule you as an adult is unhealthy. Some people use guilt to control others, and if there's someone in your life who tries to guilt you into making certain decisions, they are not a person you want on your board of directors.

Before Isaiah, I never knew you could veto someone's influence, so I was surprised when my choice to say no worked out for me. Isaiah and I still played basketball, but he found another young guy on our street who shared his enthusiasm for mischief. Meanwhile, I fell in with the punk rock kids at my school, who all wore flannel shirts, listened to grunge music, and watched Quentin Tarantino movies. In my new friends, I gained a different source of influence for music, movies, and beliefs. At the time, I didn't realize I was vetoing Isaiah's ideas in favor of others, but I had begun to curate what I allowed to influence me and appreciated the value of discretion.

Years later, during my employment at H-E-B, I was working the checkout line when I saw Isaiah walk into the store. Seeing him shocked me because, while we had fallen out of touch, I'd heard through neighborhood gossip that he'd been in prison. When I walked up to Isaiah, he looked like a kid who had just woken from a coma, with the biggest smile on his face as he gave me a hug. He said the prison had handed him a fifty-dollar check and a bus ticket, then released him that day.

As soon as he said that, I immediately wondered what a man, freshly released from prison, would want to buy first at the grocery store. Not only what would he buy, but what would I buy if I were in his position? I subtly looked into Isaiah's shopping basket as we made small talk, and I saw my answer: beer and cookie dough. After a year or two locked away, that was what he'd been craving the most.

This moment with Isaiah was humbling because, for the first time, the outcome of bad choices was standing right in front of me. I could have easily gone down the same path as Isaiah if I'd spent more time with him and hadn't vetoed his poor decisions. It could have been me, finally free from prison, holding a basket full of Sunkist and ravioli, or whatever food I'd have missed while locked away. At that moment, it had never been clearer that who my friends were mattered.

Sometimes, you can't decide who shares your time. If you have a sibling who treats you poorly or a coworker who undermines your efforts, you may not be able to avoid them, but you can always veto their ideas. Ask yourself, who in your life may be negatively influencing you? Is there anyone who routinely lowers your self-esteem, attacks your character, or bullies you? If you can name someone, it doesn't necessarily mean you have to reject that person entirely, but be discerning about how you allow their ideas to affect your worldview.

GOOD FRIENDS MAKE GOOD INFLUENCES

After attending a rough middle school, I transferred to a magnet high school called Brackenridge. Around the same time, my older sister Sonia attended the best public school in the city, a health care magnet called Health Careers High School. In a blow to my self-confidence, I didn't get accepted into Health Careers, but Sonia met with the principal of her school to advocate on my behalf. My mom brought in my report cards and every award I'd ever won, and thanks to my sister's good reputation at the school, the principal reversed my rejection. It was at Health Careers that I met my friend and board member, Dax Moreno.

If Isaiah is an example of a toxic influence, Dax is on the opposite end of the spectrum—but when I first met him, I hated him. I started attending Health Careers and fell in with a group of guys from my previous school district. One day during a basketball game, a friend of mine almost got into a fight with Dax. Being loyal to my friends, I assumed Dax was a jerk.

However, my newfound group of friends didn't last long. Several weeks into the school year, I walked into the classroom and couldn't find them. As it turned out, my friends had been caught smoking weed behind the gym and were expelled. I finished the school year mostly solo and returned after the summer to start my clinical rotation year. At Health Careers, you had to work in a hospital for a year, complete with getting inoculations, donning scrubs, and wearing terrible old-lady shoes.

During my first week of clinical rotations, I was on the bus going to the hospital with a bunch of my peers. Dax was minding his own business when a girl from our class went out of her way to pick an argument with him, and he wasn't about to roll over without defending himself. I'd written Dax off because of our previous interactions, but like Jet Li in a kung fu movie, he put the verbal smackdown on her. I was so impressed by his intellect that, in a single moment, I switched from hating Dax to wanting to be his friend. Whether or not I was explicitly aware of it, I could tell that he would be a positive influence on my life.

Around the same time, I met another board member of mine, Luke Owen, in Latin class. Like Dax, I wasn't fond of Luke at first, either. Luke would always sit next to the teacher's projector and fidget his foot until the papers fell off the machine. I didn't realize he wasn't doing it on purpose and assumed he was simply being annoying. Later, Luke proved that I'd been wrong about him and became my close friend. First impressions don't always reveal a person's character, so it's important to keep an open mind about the people you meet—the ones you least expect might change your life.

DON'T BE AFRAID TO EXPLORE YOUR OPTIONS

While surrounding yourself with the wrong people can negatively influence you, it can also help you discover the qualities in people, jobs, and circumstances that you want to avoid. For me, being immersed in the medical profession at Health Careers guided me to a life-changing decision: I didn't want a career in medicine.

I remember the day I made the decision not to work in health care. Dax and I had finished our rotations for the day and were chatting over breakfast tacos when we both admitted our true feelings about health care. Our exchange went like this:

Dax: "Man, there's not enough windows in this place. Makes it kind of depressing."

Lorenzo: "Yeah, and a lot of the nurses I work with really don't seem to like their jobs."

Dax: "You know...I don't think I want to work in medicine."

Lorenzo: "To be honest, I don't want to either."

Neither of us liked working at the hospital, but I was still shocked by how decisive Dax sounded about his rejection of the profession. He helped to validate my feelings, and I realized that I, too, could make that choice—and I did.

As a young professional, it's important for you to try different jobs before deciding on a career path. Attending Health Careers High School saved me years of effort attempting to get through college and then find a job in medicine, and it put me in the informed position to veto an entire industry. I never expected to work in technology, but it ended up being the best fit for me.

My advice to you is this: don't rush through huge life decisions like choosing a career. If you've recently graduated high school or college, you likely feel tremendous pressure to figure out what's next. Everyone expects you to know what you want to do with your life, but it's okay to spend time on the front end deciding whether an industry is right for you. If you are worried that you haven't "taken the next step," always remember that a career almost never follows a linear path.

LESSONS FROM YOUR FRIENDS

The beauty of diversity is that there's so much to learn from others' perspectives. My friends taught me many things, but what has influenced me the most is Dax's fearlessness and Luke's thirst for knowledge. Working in the hospital, I lived in fear that, one day, I would make a mistake and kill someone. Dax wasn't afraid of that at all. If the doctors had let him into the surgery room to assist with an operation, he wouldn't have hesitated—he was fearless.

Luke, on the other hand, never stopped exploring the world. He would learn everything there was to know about a subject and then move on to the next. My modus operandi was a bit different. I was comfortable not knowing the answer to a question, whereas Luke would spend his whole lunch hour in the library reading just to find the answer to a question someone randomly asked. Before you wonder, this was pre-Google, so guys like us had to actually go and research info in books. #OldSchool

Dax and Luke were so different from one another and from me. As I mentioned in the previous chapter, you want that kind of diversity on your board of directors. It's your job to surround yourself with a variety of people and discern which values to adopt from them. The friend who can hold their tongue, the friend who's patient, the friend who has great listening skills—these are the friends that should influence you.

While you think about who influences you, take a minute to also consider whom *you* influence. Friendships involve an exchange of energy. If your friend feels sad and you comfort them, they're withdrawing from you and vice versa. A problem, or power imbalance, occurs when one person acts as a leech and withdraws without ever depositing energy. Always be the friend who deposits. If someone constantly gives you advice and spends energy trying to make your life better, make sure that you reciprocate. Ask how they're doing or give them feedback on their problems. Sometimes, the best way to deposit energy into a friendship is simply by listening.

FRIENDS WILL CHANGE YOUR LIFE

The people you hang out with will change your life for better or worse. In my case, Dax is the person who introduced me to the IT industry. I had just been promoted to the produce department at H-E-B, which was a huge step up from being a bagger. Working in produce was my first brush with arrogance—the produce guys were cool and wore the latest and greatest Nikes; plus, I got my own apron and box cutter. I thought I was real hot shit.

One day, Dax called me at the grocery store. This was before cell phones, so I answered the store's telephone—an old-fashioned wall model by today's standards—and stretched the curly cord all the way from the main floor into the back room. Dax told me he'd started working at Gateway and was crushing his sales quota. When his boss asked if he had any friends who worked as hard as him, he said, "Yes, my friend Lorenzo." Dax wanted me to come in for an interview, but I had just gotten my promotion at H-E-B. I basically told him, "Dude, that's the stupidest idea ever. I don't know anything about computers." That's the reason I gave Dax, but in my mind, I was saying, *Do you have any idea how fresh the cilantro is this season?*

Despite my rejection of his offer, Dax didn't give up. For the next two weeks, he called me every other day and harassed me to take the opportunity, like any good friend and board member should. Dax had people skills for days—he could sell a total stranger a product they didn't even need. He was also an incredibly effective salesperson, whereas I was so shy, I hated paying for gum at the cash register. He sold me on the fact that the tech industry had potential, I would receive a raise of $0.25, and the job wasn't manual labor. Finally, he convinced me to come into Gateway for an interview.

I was afraid to take a job I knew nothing about, but Dax helped me overcome my fear and anxiety. A good board member will always explain things to you, be patient with you, and walk you through difficult moments. Also, I was able to ease into the new role, because when I took the job at Gateway, I was the lowest employee on the totem pole. My job was to greet people, put their name on my clipboard, answer phones, and clean the store. I wasn't ready to be a salesperson like Dax, but the role enabled me to learn about computers for the first time.

Several years later, Gateway wanted to promote me to a sales position. I knew in my heart that I wouldn't be good at sales, so I got out of it by convincing them to hire Luke instead. Luke was already a master at computers and was perfect for the role. Eventually, my manager wanted to promote me again, and I couldn't avoid it a second time. For about a year, I was Gateway's absolute worst salesperson and never hit my goals.

Around that time, Gateway partnered with OfficeMax and, in a terrible business move, opened small showrooms in the office supply stores. Being the worst salesperson, my boss exiled me to the OfficeMax location, where I was one of the only Gateway employees in the store. The move worked out to my benefit; I almost never had to interact with customers and spent a lot of my time reading on the Internet and becoming familiar with technology. After struggling in a typing class in high school, I took the time to learn how to type properly. While the sales role afforded me plenty of free time, I knew my job at Gateway had no real future.

One day, I received a call from my good friend James Brehm, the first professional salesperson I'd ever met. He had recently left Gateway to work at Rackspace as one of their first ten sales guys and wanted me to join him there. I remember how he first described the company to me: "It's a tiny startup downtown, and it probably won't last. Really, it might go out of business, *but* it's a fun place to work, and every week they buy food for the whole company, whatever you want to eat."

In retrospect, his description is funny because Rackspace grew into a two-billion-dollar publicly traded company. However, we had no idea the business would pan out that way back then, and I'd be lying if I said the free lunch didn't help sell me on the job. So I interviewed, got the job, and moved from Gateway to Rackspace with all the same fears I'd had during my earlier transition. Once again, having my personal board of directors helped me cope. Switching jobs was a bit easier the second time; the feelings of fear and uncertainty were no longer unfamiliar, and I knew my board members had my back.

I almost didn't take the job, because before formally deciding to go to Rackspace, I encountered a very odd dilemma. When I informed my Gateway coworkers that I was leaving, one of them confronted me and said, "You can't go work at Rackspace! It's a porn shop and you go to church. I can't believe you're even thinking about it!" Of course, James assured me that, while, yes, the Internet did have pornography, it was a tiny percentage of what Rackspace hosted. I had a feeling in my gut that Rackspace wasn't a sinister company, and after consulting with my board members, I decided to take the job.

I'll never forget the day I received my offer letter. I was sitting at OfficeMax making $8.75 an hour when I read that Rackspace was offering me the role of account manager, level one, with a base salary of thirty thousand dollars, plus commissions. I'd only ever heard of being a salaried employee before and couldn't believe it—if I accidentally went ten minutes over my lunch break, I'd still receive the same paycheck? I felt as though I'd pulled one over on the company and they'd forgotten to ask if I had a college degree. I promised myself that I'd work tirelessly to earn my keep and never take my job for granted.

With the move to Rackspace, I'd taken a huge step up in my career, and it never would've happened if I'd chosen different people to be my friends and board members. Every person you let into your life offers you different paths of possibilities, and all those years ago, if I'd chosen Isaiah, my path might have led to jail. My advice to you is to choose your friends wisely, because who you hang out with will affect your life for a long time to come.

CRUSHES ARE NOT MENTORS

"A mentor is someone who believes in your potential."

—GRAHAM WESTON

The first "guy crush" I ever had was on a coworker at Handy Andy, the grocery store where I had my first job. I worked as a bagger alongside all sorts of different personalities. Some coworkers kept their demeanor strictly business, while others acted like themselves and had a fun time. Then there were guys like David.

David was a Hispanic guy from my neighborhood with long hair, glasses, and a smile that would charm pretty girls and old ladies alike. He was a tough, stocky guy, and there was a swagger to his step that made him look like a bulldog when he walked. I'd often see him stroll by while I was waiting for my parents to pick me up from work. David would tell funny stories and was always nice to me, so I thought he was the coolest guy in the world. Like Isaiah, David was completely different from me and had qualities I wished I possessed.

I had such a guy crush on David that I'd always try to bag in his lane when he was working the cash register. I'd even hide in the dog food aisle, which was always empty, and mimic David's bulldog walk, complete with closed, swinging fists and a scowl. I thought walking like him would make me a smidge tougher, but who was I kidding? I was desperate to be as cool and charming as him.

At the peak of my admiration for him, David told me a story while I bagged groceries in his checkout lane. Handy Andy wasn't a particularly reputable store, so David would usually ignore the customers and continue telling his story while he rung them up. That day, his story was about a guy with a grudge and was especially profanity laden, but he didn't hesitate to keep spouting cusses when an elderly lady walked up to his register with her food-stamp check and two baskets of groceries. For the sake of keeping this conversation PG-13, I'll replace David's favorite four-letter word with "effing."

David narrated his story to the rhythm of the scanner *beeps* as he rang up the groceries, and it went something like this:

"So there was this dude I was keeping an eye on for a long time—*beep*—and I was at this party where he was talking shit to me—*beep*—but I didn't get to kick his ass at this party 'cause all of his homeboys were there, right?—*beep, beep, beep*—So one day, I'm riding the bus to go see my old lady—*beep*—and when the bus pulls up off Hildebrand, I see that dude sitting at the bus stop!—*beep*—So I say to myself, 'Awe yeah it's on baby'—*beep*—Then I yelled, 'Bus driver, stop the effing bus!'—*beep, beep, beep*—So the bus driver stops, right? I jump out, and he doesn't even see it coming—*beep*—and boom! I kick him right in the effing face!—*beep*—And I'm all, you wanna talk shit now, huh, *puto*?—*beep*—I effing roll him up good, dude—*beep, beep, beep*—So, I kick his ass, right? And then I jump back on the bus—*beep*—It was crazy, dude."

As David finished ringing up this poor old lady's groceries, he turned to her and, like flipping a switch, said with a straight face, "Ma'am, your total will be $94.68."

I giggled like a schoolgirl throughout David's story and thought he was so cool because he didn't care about impressing people the way I did, but there was a problem. I slowly realized over time that David was an awesome guy crush, but he wouldn't make a good mentor because he wasn't going anywhere. David had been fixing up an old muscle car for years, saying that things would be better in his life when it was finished, but he was never going to finish it. He had dreams and aspirations, but no ambition, no drive, and no plan.

WORK ALWAYS COMES FIRST

David made work fun, but he wasn't someone I aspired to imitate beyond his storytelling ability. The most important lesson when choosing whom to associate with at work is to not get intoxicated by the fun. At a full-time job, you often end up spending more time with your coworkers than your own family, so it's easy to gravitate toward the people who make work a better time—the office clowns, the good storytellers, the gossips, or the people who share your hobbies. These people may make work more enjoyable, but they're also a distraction.

That's not to say that fun doesn't have its place in the office, but the fun should always reinforce the work. For example, at Rackspace, my teammates and I would throw a football around while on conference calls with clients. It was a good outlet for any stress we may have been dealing with, but it didn't distract from the work. Hard work should always build up pressure and fun is the value that releases that pressure, if done correctly. Work comes first, and that's a lesson I never would've learned from David if I'd chosen him as a mentor.

HOW TO CHOOSE A MENTOR

My first real mentor was a guy named Daniel De Leon who worked with me at H-E-B. Daniel had gone to high school with two of my older brothers and knew my whole family. He'd fill me in on little bits of my family's history that I might not have heard otherwise, like the time my brother Mark almost got into a brawl with one of the baddest *vatos*, or dudes, at school. Having that connection with Daniel made me trust him, and I felt that he looked out for me. What made Daniel different from David is that he had a plan; he attended the University of Texas at San Antonio and worked at H-E-B to pay his way through school. He talked about H-E-B as one part of his journey, rather than the end stop. Daniel made a great mentor because he wanted to show me what he'd learned and didn't hesitate to share information, even if it meant talking from check stand to check stand in between scanning customers' groceries.

One quality a great mentor needs to possess is domain expertise. Luke embodied this quality; he was a domain expert in computer technology and could explain every intricacy of the Internet. Ask yourself: who in your world knows a lot about a particular topic or field of study? You need people in your professional network who are domain experts and mentors.

Graham Weston taught me that **a mentor is someone who believes in your potential**. Often, a mentor chooses you rather than the other way around. They recognize a characteristic or talent that can be nurtured and improved, and are willing to take the time to help you. It doesn't do any good to know intelligent experts if they're unwilling to share their knowledge.

How do you know when you or someone you know is an expert? Author Malcolm Gladwell describes a concept in his book *Outliers* called the Rule of Ten Thousand. He explains that it takes ten thousand hours of doing something to become an expert in that area. When I read his book, it gave me hope, because I realized, at that point in my career, I had likely spent about ten thousand hours communicating with customers and colleagues in person, through e-mail, or on the phone. I felt empowered knowing that I had worked my way up to being an expert communicator. The people around you who are experts are the ones who have spent considerable time working in their field and could teach you things you won't learn in a textbook.

TIMES MY MENTORS HELPED ME

When I first became a manager, I had to deal with an employee who routinely showed up late. I didn't know how to approach the situation, but my first instinct was to send a passive aggressive e-mail to the entire team asking them to arrive on time in the morning. Fortunately, I didn't do that and, instead, consulted with my mentor, a woman named

Shannon Forester-Smykay, who did have ten thousand hours of management experience. She told me sending an e-mail to the team would be the worst, most demoralizing thing I could do, and that I should confront the offending employee directly. The experience made me so thankful for her guidance and really nailed home the importance of having mentors in your network.

Another time when a mentor helped me with an important career decision was two years before I moved to London. My boss at Rackspace, Anne Bowman, approached me one day and said that the London account manager was going on holiday for a month and that they needed someone to go there to fill the role. Since I had no wife or kids, I was objectively the most flexible person, and she thought I should go. I was bewildered at the idea—I had never been out of the country and had only been on a plane once before, to go to Las Vegas with my brother a couple months earlier. Anne saw my fear and walked me through getting a passport, including taking me to the post office to have my picture taken and fill out the form; then she put me on the second plane ride of my life. Being in London turned out to be a wonderful experience, and after a month flew by, I returned home. Anne saw my potential and knew the experience would change me, and it did.

Back in the San Antonio office, I had a colleague named Jake Gracia, who was like my "office big sister." We shared a cubicle, joked a lot, and became good friends. When she, an Anglo woman, married a Hispanic man named DJ Gracia, I decorated her desk with a poncho, piñata, and fiesta decorations to welcome her to the Hispanic family—that's the kind of friendship we had. Before she was my mentor, I actually had the chance to mentor her a bit. When she started at Rackspace, she was well versed in the world but didn't know much about managed hosting. I remember pulling my computer apart and walking her through all of the different hardware and terms she needed to know. It went like this: "That is a processor, and it's like the engine in your car." Just like someone had done for me a couple of years earlier, I was able to explain computers to Jake, but the way she influenced my life was much more drastic.

Every quarter, the managing director of the London office, Dominic Monkhouse, would visit for leadership meetings. He'd come by the cubicle Jake and I shared and ask if I would come back to work in the London office long-term. Every time, I'd turn him down. One day, after I turned down Dominic, Jake looked at me and said, "What the hell is wrong with you?"

I told her, "Look, I was in London, and it's cool, but my family is here, and my friends are here. My parents would be mad if I left. Why would I move to the UK?"

Jake looked me dead in the eyes and said, "You're being an

idiot. You need to go work in that London office, because living abroad is going to change the way you look at the world. When you come back, everybody's going to be hanging out at the same bar, talking about the same things, and doing the same stuff they're doing now. You're not going to miss a thing."

Jake picked up on my biggest fear, which was the fear of missing out, and told me exactly what I needed to hear. I remember being shocked and thinking, *That actually makes a lot of sense.* I went home and told my parents I planned to move to the UK, and as I suspected, they were pissed, but I decided to go for it. I'm so glad I did, because living in London was one of the greatest experiences of my life. I traveled the world and met new people, all because one mentor recognized my potential and saw what I could gain by taking a risk.

WHEN YOU DON'T KNOW EXPERTS

If you don't have an expert to tap for advice, even someone with six months or a year more experience than you can be incredibly helpful. You never know what wisdom they may have gained in that time until you ask. Another option is finding a virtual mentor, someone you've met and communicated with remotely. You can even have a mentor you've never met before at all. An expert in your field might author a blog, host a podcast, or run a YouTube channel—there are many places you can find and reach out to experts from all over the world.

Two people I've never met fill the virtual mentor role for me: a Presbyterian theologian named Dr. Timothy Keller and author Tim Ferris. I discovered Dr. Keller through his podcast; he took an old story that I'd read in the Old Testament many times before and told it in a completely fresh way. I listened to hours and hours of his podcast because I was so enthralled by his different way of thinking. Tim Ferris's book The 4-Hour Workweek changed my views on the workplace and productivity. Reading his book was one of the first times I was so hooked by the content that I couldn't absorb it fast enough. That's what mentors do—they change your worldview and make you excited to learn.

In addition to thinking about other people, consider the areas in which *you* might be considered an expert. Even if you have mentors and experts in your life, never stop striving to be one yourself. If you haven't put ten thousand hours toward any one endeavor, don't worry. Think about where you *are* focusing your time and energy. Is there something that people ask you to help them with? Something that you seem to do a little bit better than the rest? Whatever that skill is, figure it out and double down. Don't focus on your weaknesses, because you will never be world-class at them. Instead, put your time and effort into the things you have a natural ability in and the Rule of Ten Thousand will take over.

SECTION II

UNDERSTANDING HOW BUSINESS WORKS

IT'S NOT WHAT YOU KNOW, BUT WHO

"Reputation is a currency."

—DANNY GOMEZ JR.

My first official job was being a bagger at the Handy Andy grocery store, but that doesn't mean it was the first time I ever worked. Before I earned a paycheck, I worked for my father. He was an X-ray technician by trade, but he built houses on the side. He knew how to do it all—the carpentry, the electrical work, the plumbing—and as a result, as soon as my brothers and I were old enough to hold a hammer, we worked with him.

My father built the house I grew up in and our neighbor's house, among others, which required a lot of time and effort. All of my childhood weekends were spent helping my father build houses from the ground up. We did everything from digging foundation holes and hanging Sheetrock to hammering shingles. Admittedly, I hated it.

Digging holes in the Texas summer heat was not easy. My brothers and I had a process figured out: one of us would pour water on the ground to loosen the soil while the others attacked the rock-hard dirt with pickaxes and shovels. There were small frustrations as well; every time my three brothers and I needed hammers, there always seemed to be only two.

I have a vivid memory of driving up to an empty lot that my parents bought. They planned to construct an apartment building and had stuck stakes in the ground to indicate where the foundation holes needed to be dug. My stomach sank to unforeseen depths when I saw nearly a hundred stakes littered across the property. I felt like part of a chain gang digging those holes, but my brother Danny gave me great advice that day. He told me to get another job—any job— as soon as I turned sixteen, and that would be my ticket out.

As much as I loathed the manual labor, building houses set the lifelong tone for my work ethic. Once you've dug a hundred five-foot deep holes, any other work feels easy in comparison. For example, when I became a bagger at the grocery store, nothing about the work phased me. I carried my family's strong work ethic with me to every job from there on out.

As I mentioned before, working hard was my family's legacy, and laziness was a major sin. Being called lazy by my parents was one of the worst insults they could give someone. My father would always relate laziness back to a story about the downfall of Kelly Air Force Base, a military installation near where I grew up in San Antonio. My dad said people called the base "Kelly Jelly," because anything went and there were no rules. The union representing the workers was so strong that the employees believed the officials would never close the base. As a result, an atmosphere of laziness developed. Workers would start drinking at noon, slack off, and cut corners. One time, they even lost a jet engine that later turned up for sale in a classified ad. Now keep in mind, I am sure not everyone at Kelly was lazy, but to my father, the few bad apples (PLU code #4016) had spoiled the whole bunch.

I'm sure you can guess what happened—the base closed. There was outrage and picketing, but it was done. My father would tell this story, shake his head, and say, "That's the end result of laziness." I didn't realize it as a kid, but he was warning my siblings and I to never associate with people who lack a strong work ethic. Laziness tends to spread between coworkers, and if you spend time with lazy people, they can drag you down with them.

YOUR CONNECTIONS ARE A REFLECTION OF YOU

Principle II explored how your peers influence you; this principle is about how your choice of peers influences others. For example, if you associate with lazy people, you'll wind up in their camp and earn yourself a bad brand. It doesn't matter if you're not lazy; people will jump to conclusions— conclusions that are hard to undo.

On the other hand, if you associate with hard workers, you'll be branded a hard worker. The people in my life boosted my reputation, which benefited me tremendously, even as early as my first paid job. By the time I was sixteen, I knew digging holes wasn't the job for me, and I began applying to every business within a one-mile radius of my house. I reached out to all the fast-food chains and grocery stores, but didn't hear a response from any of them. McDonalds, Burger King, Pizza Hut, I would have taken a job anywhere.

All the rejection made me feel pretty bad about myself, but then I realized I was an unknown quantity—just a random person walking in with no flashy skills, no references, and no way to leave a lasting impression. On top of that, I was a shy kid who didn't know how to sell myself to potential employers. I eventually got an interview with the Handy Andy grocery store, but it wasn't on my own merit. I was asked to come in because my older brother Hector had a rock star reputation as a hard worker back when he worked there. He called the manager, and right away, the manager agreed to give me an interview.

At that point, I realized your reputation, or the reputation of people you know, is a currency. My brother's reputation was able to buy me an interview. From that point forward, it was my responsibility to make a good impression, but Hector got me in the door. I wore my nicest pair of Dickies and walked into the grocery store with a folder of my report cards; I had no idea what to expect at an interview. However, as soon as I sat down with the manager, I quickly realized that none of what I thought was important mattered.

My interview was with a stern man named Mr. Diaz, who was as wide as he was tall and wore a finely manicured mustache. Our conversation went exactly like this:

"So, you're Hector Gomez's brother?"

"Yes, sir."

"Do you work hard like your brother?"

"Yes, sir."

"Okay, you've got the job. You start on Monday."

That exceedingly brief exchange was my entire first interview, and it clearly illustrated how true this principle is: **it's not what you know, but who you know**. Nearly every job I've started since then has been an iteration of the same story, where someone else has put their reputation on the line for me. Now that I am a little further into my career, I make a point to pay it forward and put my reputation on the line for others.

As a young professional, you need to think about how you can build your reputation. Think about how you're building it every single day, even every hour, at work. Do you slack off? Are you the person playing ping pong all the time or the one taking smoke breaks constantly? Or are you the person who comes in, puts their head down, and cranks out the work because you want a good reputation?

One way or another, you're going to get a reputation. It's just a matter of what reputation you're going to get. I was lucky to inherit my family's reputation of being hard workers, which started by my grandparents working as migrant workers and continued by my parents building houses. My siblings and I felt a duty to continue our family's legacy and followed through on it. Fortunately, you don't need a legacy to build a good reputation. Whether you come from the hood or don't have an education, if you have drive and ambition, hard work is a social currency anyone can earn.

HOW TO BUILD YOUR REPUTATION

If you want to build a good reputation, there are several tactical things you can do. First, you want to be one of the best people at your given role. I know I just said that it's not what you know, but eventually what you know will matter. This means that once your foot is in the door, you better learn everything there is to know about that job. Think of it as being in the top percentile—better than 90 percent of your peers. For example, if you're a grocery store bagger, you want to be one of the top three baggers in your store. This strategy worked to keep me motivated when I was a bagger. I'd put my head down and aim to be the fastest and most accurate bagger on the line. I wanted to be the person the cashiers preferred on their check stand and the employee who earned the most compliments from customers. Simply put, aim to be the best.

Later, when I was promoted to cashier, I redefined my goals. I wanted to be the cashier who never gave inaccurate change or had money missing from my till. I also memorized nearly all of the produce PLU (Price Look Up) codes, which is a big deal when you are a cashier. To this day, I still remember that Chiquita bananas are #4011, but the cheaper bananas are #4237. I learned that any produce that is organic has a 9 in front of the normal code, but we never really got organic stuff at my store. Only fancy people ate organic. The only reason I remember cantaloupe is #4049 is because it reminded me of a scene from the movie *True Romance*.

Christopher Walken calls Dennis Hopper a cantaloupe right before he blows his brains out. I always quoted that line in my head and would remember the produce code whenever I scanned the fruit.

Each time I've changed jobs, I've given myself new goals that fit the role. You want to be a detective when it comes to acing your job so that you know which skills to improve. As a young professional, you should ask yourself: what is it that I do and how can I be the best?

Look around your department and assign a grade to your fellow employees. Who goes far beyond the minimum requirements of their job? Who earns an A, B, C, D, or F? Once you've thought about who makes a good role model, copy those A-rated people. Learn their tricks and associate with them. Remember, A-players roll with other A-players.

I've mentioned this before, but to build a good reputation, you have to work hard, and working hard means putting in the hours. If that requires coming in early and leaving late, so be it. If it means you need to educate yourself further and learn about a subject or skill, you'd better do it. Working hard means doing more than is required of you, and it always takes time. In the same way you can't get a car without first saving money, you can't take a shortcut to earn a good reputation. The following story from my family illustrates the point about shortcuts in a way that even my young, teenage self understood.

After I started earning a paycheck at Handy Andy, I knew what I wanted to spend my money on: a car. I had to get dropped off and picked up from work, but having my own car would mean freedom. Specifically, I wanted a 1967 Mustang, just like the guys from the movie *The Outsiders*. I remember my brother telling me how, when he was my age, he received an interesting phone call from one of our uncles. For context, our uncle lived in Laredo and worked a variety of interesting jobs, which included loan-sharking for Las Vegas casinos, among others. Generally, he was a pretty scary dude and said *vato* after everything.

One day, my uncle called my brother and said, "Listen, I know you're looking for a car, *vato*. Well, I got a car here and it's free, but you need to pick it up tonight. You gotta pick it up tonight; then tomorrow you gotta paint that shit. It used to belong to a big drug dealer in Laredo, but don't worry, it's legit. It's not stolen or anything, but you need to come get it tonight, and tomorrow you gotta paint that shit."

The car was a Camaro IROC-Z—a dream car for most teenagers back in his day—and my brother, being a naive sixteen-year-old, only registered one thing: free car. My brother went to our father and said, "Hey, Pops, Tio's got a free car down in Laredo."

Our father just shot him a look and replied, "Are you serious right now? There's absolutely no way we're taking that car. No way."

My brother called our uncle back to politely decline the offer, but our uncle was vexed. He said, "But it's for free, *vato*. It's a free car. Free! All you gotta do is pick it up right now and paint it tomorrow."

He swore the car wasn't stolen, but our father was resolute; if an offer seems too good to be true, it probably is. Whether you're talking about getting a car or earning a reputation, there are no shortcuts.

Working hard means putting in the time, but it also means acting with a sense of urgency. Your customers and boss don't want to wait for you to solve their problems, and a hard worker will try to minimize delays as much as possible. Part of cutting down on lost time is being assertive and not always waiting to be told what to do.

When I worked as a bagger, one of the tasks that everyone tried to avoid was rounding up the baskets in the parking lot. Other employees would try to make excuses, talk their way out of it, or delay the inevitable, asking things like, "How about after lunch?" or "Can I wait until it's cloudier outside?" My peers' reluctance was understandable—collecting baskets in an asphalt parking lot during a Texas summer is really unpleasant, like 110-degrees-in-the-shade unpleasant—but giving anything other than a quick agreement will leave a bad impression on your boss.

After my experience digging holes for my father, rounding up baskets was child's play in comparison. I'd say to myself, "This is easy. I'm going to get it done and be back in the air-conditioning within twenty minutes." Most tasks, when you analyze them, aren't that bad, and it's easy to psych yourself up to do them. If you adopt an agreeable attitude when your boss asks you to do an unpopular job, you can impress them with your genuine willingness to help. Even better, do the task before they ask.

Another key part of building a reputation is managing your brand. When you get considered for a promotion, you don't want someone to say, "That person is immature." As soon as someone with influence speaks badly about you, you've lost your shot. Your brand is one of the hardest professional commodities to manage, because once you've earned a negative label, it's almost impossible to change. Negativity sticks to you like melted wax in your hair. When that happens, there's nothing left to do but shave your head. In the workplace, this often translates into finding a new job.

Even if you switch employers, never underestimate the small size of the world. Industries, even global ones, are tight-knit, and everyone talks. If you burn a bridge with one person, there's a good chance you'll cross paths with them or someone they know again. Never assume you can tell someone off without it coming back to haunt you—blemishes on your reputation always return.

Not only will the people who cross your path remember you, but keep in mind that you're always networking. You never know who could help you down the line. As I described in a previous chapter, my friend Dax's reputation helped me get a job at Gateway, and I helped get Luke a job, and so on. Then my friend James Brehm took a job at Rackspace, where he recruited me and a whole posse of connections to join him. It's this cascade effect that makes the choice of who you network with so important.

If you have a good reputation and a willingness to help your network, your connections will pay it forward. If you have a great reputation, people will seek you out for their network, and you'll be able to pick and choose who you connect with the most. Choose wisely, and your professional companions will take you with them as they progress up the corporate ladder.

DEFINING YOUR REPUTATION

If you're not sure what your reputation is now, take a good, hard look at yourself. Are you the person who always comes up with a reason why something won't work? If so, you might be too negative. Instead, try to always suggest a solution. If you give one reason for shooting someone's idea down, give two alternatives in its place. The person who only has bad things to say is one of the most common brands I see, and you never want to be that person.

Another common brand is the old-timer who is stuck in their ways and refuses to change. If your coworkers are making a plan, you don't want them to exclude you because they think you won't be agreeable to change. You won't be invited to work on innovative projects, and your career growth will be terribly stinted. Eventually, people with the old-timer brand are often perceived as irrelevant and are among the first employees struck from the roster during a layoff. Always be the person who's open to new ideas.

If you do earn a bad reputation, you're not hopeless, but you *will* be fighting an uphill battle. The best thing you can do is manage your brand before it goes sour in the first place. It's significantly easier to build a good brand than it is to undo a negative one.

REPUTATION AS CURRENCY

As I mentioned before, reputation acts as a sort of social and professional currency. Reputation can sometimes open doors better than any money, degree, or experience—it's incredibly valuable. If someone with a good reputation is willing to vouch for you, you can purchase opportunities with their currency. Similarly, if there's someone who you would endorse, you can use your good reputation to help them. Often, this exchange results in a favor trade, but it shouldn't be undertaken lightly.

If someone vouches for you, your subsequent performance reflects on their reputation. Nobody is going to risk their brand on you if they think you'll make them look bad. For example, if I had shown up late to work, slacked off, or bad-mouthed employees after my brother Hector helped me get the job at Handy Andy, my actions would have damaged his reputation. The next time Hector recommended someone to the grocery manager, the manager probably wouldn't trust Hector's judgment.

A while back, a leader who reported to me hired three employees from his previous job. Each one was a rock star, but one young girl in particular was bursting with talent. She hit the ground running and everyone loved her. A few months in, however, she was struggling to get along with a coworker and secretly started looking for another job. Not even six months in, she put in her notice. We were shocked she didn't give her leader a chance to fix the situation. Even worse, she was going to a job where she wouldn't be getting better skills or opportunities than what we were giving her, just a marginal pay raise.

On her last week, I pulled her aside and gave her some feedback. I said, "I'll never stop anyone from doing something they think will better themselves, but I need to tell you that your manager vouched for you when he brought you over to us. Because you're leaving so soon, you've eroded his credibility. Now, when he makes a recommendation, people are going to second-guess him. You've cost his reputation some currency, and I want you to know that. I hope you crush it at your next job, but there is someone at your new gig vouching for you, and if you do this again, you will erode that person's credibility too." Remember, your actions don't just affect you.

When you progress in your career, there will come a day when someone asks you for a letter of recommendation. My suggestion is to think long and hard about saying yes. When you sign that letter, you're attaching your name to the recipient, and you want to make sure only to give that gift to people you know will honor their responsibility. If you know the person is an honest, hard worker, absolutely endorse them. When good endorsements happen, everyone's social currency rises.

BUILDING YOUR REPUTATION FROM THE GROUND UP

When you're just starting out in your career, your reputation is a blank canvas, and it's up to you to make it remarkable. Think about who you could call if you needed someone to vouch for you during an interview. Who can attest to the skills you possess? If you have a hard time thinking of anyone, you have some work to do to build your reputation.

One of the best things you can do to jumpstart your career is start building skills, but being skilled won't get you nearly as far if you have a negative brand. When I started my job at Rackspace, I worked hard but didn't manage my reputation. While the people who knew me the best were aware of my hard work—I was on the highest performing team that year and always hit my numbers—to everyone else, I looked like the funny office clown.

This one, little negative association of being "the funny guy" hurt me, and I ended up getting passed over for promotions for several years. Regrettably, I didn't handle the rejection well. I was disappointed and began to develop a bad attitude, adding to my negative brand. When I moved to London for the first time, I started a weekly drinking event with a buddy of mine from Texas. We'd get together on Thursday nights and drink England's worst tequila. After a while, other coworkers joined in, and Tequila Thursday became a huge event. The situation escalated to the point where the Rackspace board of directors had a meeting about how our event was disrupting productivity; everyone was coming into the office Friday morning hungover from our event. The leaders of the London office tried to get me to cancel Tequila Thursdays, but I was having too much fun sticking it to "the man" and didn't listen. I left London with the brand of a hard-partying office clown with a bad attitude.

My reputation didn't begin to change until I moved to London for the second time. I had carried all my emotional baggage with me between the London and San Antonio Rackspace offices, but that second time crossing the sea, I decided to have a good attitude. My friend Khaled pulled me aside and advised me to move Tequila Thursday to Friday and to ask my boss for permission before reinstating the event. Before, the mere suggestion would have sent me into a rage stroke, but I swallowed my mountain of pride and asked my boss for his blessing.

I was so grateful for how graciously my boss accepted my olive branch; he recognized my attempt at maturity, and we were able to move forward. I began to reclaim my brand by making a better effort to connect and communicate with my team, to support my coworkers, and to offer positive solutions. When I returned to the United States, I was promoted to a team-leader position.

I was astonished by the effect my positive attitude had achieved. It took me five years to realize I had a problem, and once I'd figured it out, only a month to change it. I'm not necessarily saying that it'll only take one month to undo any negative reputations you may have, but I hope I can save you five years of trouble by showing you where to start.

STAND OUT FROM THE COMPETITION

"Be so good they can't ignore you."

—STEVE MARTIN

My first paid job was at Handy Andy, but Handy Andy wasn't my first choice of workplace. I wanted to work at the winning grocery store, H-E-B, which was, by far, the nicer store, closer to my house, and the place where all my brothers worked. The quote by Fred Reichheld, a man who wrote the book on customer service, and Graham Weston, who made it the mantra for Rackspace, described my desire to work at H-E-B: **"Everybody wants to be a valued member of a winning team on an inspiring mission**."

H-E-B wasn't just the winning grocery store in my neighborhood; they dominated the entire South Texas region and Mexico. When I worked at Number Five, I would sometimes pick up extra hours at another H-E-B location at Thousand Oaks and Jones Maltsberger, which was in a more affluent part of town. It was a beautiful store, and the produce manager, an older Hispanic man named Eddie, was always kind to me.

One of the first things I noticed at Thousand Oaks was that none of their intercom announcements were in Spanish. My neighborhood had a larger Hispanic population, so my local store, Number Five, often used Spanish. I quickly realized that language was one way the store differentiated itself from others. The second thing I noticed was the utter lack of jalapeños (#4693).

At the end of my shift on my first day at Thousand Oaks, I nearly flew into a panic when I realized I hadn't stocked the jalapeños. At my local store, that oversight would've been a huge sin. People bought jalapeños so fast that the produce clerks had to fill the display nearly every hour. That day, I hadn't restocked them once during my entire shift. I sprinted back onto the produce floor and frantically searched for the jalapeno display. At Number Five, the jalapeños were stocked on a huge table, but the display at Thousand Oaks made my jaw drop. At first, I couldn't even find it because I was looking at all the large displays. Then I saw it, buried deep in their vegetable section: one sad little tray of jalapeños.

I was baffled, but then it hit me: no one in that neighborhood ate jalapeños in mass quantities like they did in mine. Mind blown. The attention to detail required specializing the inventory for a particular neighborhood, and it left me feeling wildly impressed; it gave H-E-B a huge competitive advantage. Kroger came to town, but it couldn't compete. Walmart opened a location with cheaper prices, but it couldn't outperform H-E-B, either.

Many years later, I moved back into the H-E-B Number Five neighborhood. The grocery store's stock alone was enough to tell me how the neighborhood had changed in my absence. When I worked there, the prayer candle aisle was massive. When I moved back, it was a quarter of what it had been, and where the candles had shrunk, the wine aisle expanded. My point is that H-E-B did an excellent job of standing out from the competition, and that's why it came out on top.

Their tactics were simple but incredibly effective: differentiation and specialization. Every H-E-B location was customized to the point where competitors couldn't outperform them. Whenever a new H-E-B opened, their team would study its specific neighborhood: What do the people in the neighborhood eat? What is their cultural background? What do they need?

It didn't matter that H-E-B wasn't the cheapest grocery store in the area. There was always a store that was cheaper and always one that was more expensive, but H-E-B always had what their customers needed. A store looked different depending on its neighborhood. For example, if an H-E-B was in a historic part of town, their building would fit that architectural style. They went to great lengths to stand out as the local underdog business. As a result, the people of San Antonio took pride in shopping there.

WHEN YOU'RE ON THE LOSING TEAM

When I worked at Handy Andy, I felt like it was, undeniably, the losing team. H-E-B bought A-level produce, while Handy Andy only ever stocked B or C. It was a lower-tier store, and the worst part was I felt like all the other employees looked sad and defeated.

I desperately wanted to be on the winning team, and I want to point out a few reasons why you should want to be on a winning team, too. The winning team naturally recruits employees who are winners themselves, which means when you join their team, there are people who can teach you. The best people work at the best places, and you want to be around them. Winning teams are where you'll meet the mentors and, as you can probably guess, I left Handy Andy without a single mentor.

Being on a winning team will also boost your confidence. If you grew up in the hood, or were the oddball growing up, or were the child of divorced parents, you're constantly used to seeing people lose. Personally, I saw a lot of my peers drop out of school, go to jail, or head down other unfortunate paths. When you're so used to seeing people lose, you get desperate for change. I wanted so badly to see a glimmer of winning, which is why I wanted to get away from Handy Andy.

NOBODY IS EXEMPT FROM THE PROCESS

After I'd been working at Handy Andy for about a year, my sister came to me one day and told me about an upcoming H-E-B job fair. I was a bit wary—I'd already been rejected from H-E-B and didn't know how much my self-esteem could handle—but I ended up attending. I remember walking up to the table with my sister Sonia with my application in hand. I half-expected something similar to my hiring experience at Handy Andy, where someone would say, "Oh, you're Sonia Gomez's brother? Let me put your application in the special pile over here."

Unfortunately, that didn't happen. I assumed I couldn't rely on my sister's excellent reputation to open doors that time, but I listed her name on the referral section of the application anyway. To my surprise, a week later, I received a phone call from H-E-B. I realized having my sister as a connection did help me, but I still had to go through the process.

Handy Andy had no real hiring process that I could discern,

but winning teams, like H-E-B, often do. I had to go through the process of submitting an application, but Principle IV still applied: it's not what you know, but who you know. My sister had already spoken to someone about my application, and unbeknownst to me, they had put a figurative star next to my name.

I was beyond thrilled to have a chance with the winning team. After passing my interview, I went to orientation, where I was tested on basic math, identifying products, and using the cash register. I learned to separate the detergent from the frozen foods and not to squish the bread, bananas, or tomatoes. During all of this, I felt like a million bucks—I'd made it in the universe. Not only did I feel better about myself, but working at H-E-B was a vastly better experience than I'd had at Handy Andy.

Winning teams need to stand out from the competition to recruit the best people. They have different cultures, different pay, and different processes, and are constantly redefining themselves in order to stay on top. Even small details can make being on a winning team radically different from being on the losing team. H-E-B had a distinct culture and language. Employees talked about the number of their store—in my case, H-E-B Number Five—like it was their alma mater, and we weren't called employees; we were called partners. My family members who worked at H-E-B would bring this language home with them, so long before I started working there, I knew I wanted to be part of the club.

The little details are what made working at H-E-B a special experience. It was the company's way of saying, "You're part of the team." These are just a few examples of winning characteristics that I noticed at H-E-B, but many of them apply across the corporate landscape. A common culture, language, competitive pay, and exclusivity are all signs you're on the winning team.

HOW YOU CAN STAND OUT FROM THE COMPETITION

To outshine your competition in the workplace, you want to apply the H-E-B model of specialization and differentiation to yourself. My boss of many years, Graham Weston, likes to say that everyone is in sales, and if you're not selling a product, you're selling yourself and your ideas.

Specializing in a few skills can be an excellent selling point. Think about what you have a knack for and how you can master those skills. The goal is to be the go-to person in your office or professional network. For example, I was great at processing refunds. If any coworkers had trouble with a refund, they came to me. Making yourself indispensable automatically puts you ahead of the less-specialized competition.

Differentiation is when you do something that sets you apart from everybody else. During my time at H-E-B, I differentiated myself entirely by accident. Every time I had the opening produce shift, I'd come to the store at 5:00 a.m. to break down the enormous pallet of fresh fruits and vegetables for that day. After that, I'd remove any produce that had gone bad from the displays and replace it with the new inventory.

One day, I was putting out a couple cases of lettuce on a square table. I had my routine memorized by that point and could go through the motions while getting lost in my thoughts. I had set out the third case of lettuce when I looked down and realized I'd subconsciously put the heads in a pattern and built half a pyramid. For a pile of lettuce, it looked quite cool. I had a few more cases of lettuce in the back and decided to finish what I'd started.

A while later, I'd successfully built a geometrically perfect pyramid of lettuce. I stood before it as though admiring a piece of art, and if social media had existed back then, you better believe a photo of that pyramid would've been my profile picture. Not a minute later, while I was still basking in its glory, a little old lady came up and started plucking heads of lettuce from the pyramid and tossing them aside because she wasn't happy with any of them.

I was so angry, because I wanted my teammates to see the

pyramid when they came in. For the next hour, I continuously rebuilt my pyramid as an army of a hundred little old ladies tried to destroy it. Finally, my teammates arrived, and they loved it. That day, I was king of the produce section. From that point onward, whenever my boss Richard wanted to show off, he'd gather our team together and tell us, "The bosses from corporate are coming in." Then, he'd scrunch his eyebrows, shoot me a serious look, and say, "Lorenzo, build the pyramid."

The main principle in this story is differentiation. Building a pyramid of lettuce was the thing that made me special—the task only I could do. Some people can write e-mail introductions as eloquent as poetry, while other people have a magic touch for fixing the printer paper jam. What you need to do is figure out where your talents lie. What do you bring to the table? If you don't know yet, go find a way to differentiate yourself. Look for ways to build your pyramid.

LOOKS LIKE WORK, BUT ISN'T

In one of my favorite quotes, Graham Weston described a phenomenon in the workplace where someone seems like they're working, but they're not: **looks like work, but isn't**. If that describes your role, you have a problem, because everyone on a team needs to contribute in a meaningful way. But how do you know if you're adding value?

One rule for adding value I've found to be true is to always make sure you're close to the customer. As you move up the corporate ladder, the tendency is to move away from customers. For example, you might start in a call center speaking to customers all day, and then get promoted to a managerial position where you never talk to them at all. I understand why this happens—customers can be an absolute nightmare. Customers complain, they have problems, they're unreasonable, but they also pay the bills.

I've seen people in my career whose sole priority is to distance themselves from the customer, but in general, the further you are from the customer, the more expendable you are. You're the first person to be laid off when business goes poorly, but staying close to the customer is one of the best ways you can maintain job security.

The first time I encountered "looks like work, but isn't," I was working at H-E-B. The store had recently introduced a new position called "traffic controller" that all the employees wanted. When the store was at its busiest, the traffic controller would put on a bright vest and direct customers to the shortest checkout line. It was glorious, because you didn't have to deal with angry customers, help them unload their baskets, or fix problems. All you had to do was point to the shortest line.

One day, I was assigned to traffic-control duty and realized, while fun, the role was one that looked like work, but wasn't. It was an unnecessary position that wouldn't lead anywhere. A job is called work for a reason, and if you're offered a position that seems too easy or fun to be true, don't do it. Run far away, because those jobs are enjoyable for a while, until you're the first person to go.

I saw another example of "looks like work, but isn't" later in my career while working at the London Rackspace office. I became friends with a business analyst there, and one day, he vented about his job. He didn't get along with his boss and was trying to convince the company to give him a position where he'd visit all of the international offices and "build bridges."

I remember feeling kind of disgusted with his proposal: that's a fake job. What he was really telling me was that he liked to travel, and he especially liked to travel when someone else was paying for it. In no way, shape, or form did his dream job have any relevance to the customer. For me, distance from the customer is a huge red flag for a role.

As you advance in your career, don't be fooled into doing something that looks like work, but isn't. Remember that the key to adding value to a team is being close to the customer, and adding value is the number one thing you can do to maintain job security. If someone you know tells you they had to go to a golf tournament for work; just remember, "looks like work, but isn't."

HOW TO SCORE A PROMOTION

My promotion to the produce department at H-E-B was a huge deal for me. When you're seventeen years old and live in the hood, someone who's college educated with a high-and-tight haircut and a fancy title like store manager might as well be the president of the United States. One day, the manager pulled me into his office and told me I was doing a great job. He said that he noticed I had prior produce experience on my application and that he wanted to promote me.

Hearing those words was like winning the affirmation lottery. I had never been told before that I had valuable experience, and I walked a little taller that day. I credit the principle of working hard for that promotion, which compounds into another rule: **be so good they can't ignore you**.

Every day as I went into work, I'd repeat that rule to myself like a mantra. The idea is to perform your job so well that it would be a misallocation of resources for them to waste your talent in your current position rather than promote you. Promoting you is in their best interest if it means helping the company grow, bringing in more revenue, and serving more customers. Later in your career, it's fine to ask for a raise, but when you're first starting out, you should never ask for a raise or promotion. Instead, prove to your higher-ups that you deserve it.

Part of proving yourself worthy of a promotion is maintaining a positive attitude. When you're a cashier, there are three times of the year when the check stand feels like a prison more than a job: Thanksgiving Eve, Christmas Eve, and any time preceding a huge storm. In all three of these situations, everyone in the universe decides to go to the grocery store at the same time, as though a zombie apocalypse were coming and they wouldn't have another chance to buy food for a millennium. As a result, the grocery store turns into a hellish place of pandemonium and chaos.

The one silver lining of working on those days is that you could wear whatever you wanted; otherwise, a shift was eight hours of pure pain. One memorable Christmas Eve at H-E-B, I was outside collecting baskets when a manager approached me. He said they needed me on the check stand. In retrospect, that was the first signal I was performing well: my skills were too valuable to be collecting baskets.

I went to the empty check stand, put money in my till, braced myself, and turned my light on. The thing about working on Christmas Eve is, as soon as you start working the register, the line doesn't end until the moment you leave and someone replaces you. I had the unnerving feeling of being stuck in a hole and unable to dig myself out, but I put my head down and went into the zone. I decided to have an attitude so good that the bosses couldn't ignore me, and my goal was to be the fastest clerk on checkout duty that day.

I was ringing products up so fast, my check stand sounded like a machine gun: *beep, beep, beep, beep*. I knew customers didn't want to be there any more than I did, and if they saw me really hustling, they were less likely to get angry. People become unreasonable around holidays. Everyone wants to get home to their families, and as someone working in customer service, the least you can do is show you understand.

I was a man on fire, and in my mind's eye, I had smoke coming out of my check stand. At one point, several hours into my shift, I looked up and saw a thirty-something-year-old Hispanic man staring at me. He was just chuckling and nodding, and had the biggest grin on his face. He told me, "Dude, I was waiting at that check stand ten lines over, but when I saw how fast you were going, I put all my stuff back in my basket and came all the way over here." I was a little angry at him for making my line longer, but I also felt encouraged, because I had distinguished myself from the other employees. I was so efficient at ringing people up that the customers couldn't ignore me.

When you're working on Christmas Eve or in any other unpleasant situation, dragging your feet and being miserable isn't going to make the pain go away. The least you can do is have a good attitude, show a sense of urgency, and try to do your best. Make the most of an undesirable job, and with any luck, you'll earn a promotion out of it faster and with more success than if you give in to negativity.

DANCE WITH THE ONE WHO BROUGHT YOU

"There are friends who will help you move, and there are friends who will help you move a body."

—PRAVESH MISTRY

In the neighborhood where I grew up, being called disloyal was one of the worst insults you could receive. The mentality partly stemmed from the gang culture in the area. San Antonio had a bad gang problem from the 1980s into the mid-1990s, and my neighborhood was the second hottest spot in town for drive-by shootings. My father used to warn my siblings and me by saying, "When you don't have a father figure, you go and join a gang. And if you join a gang, you're going to get into trouble." Of course, that's not the outcome for most people without fathers, but his warning worked on me.

While I wasn't in a gang, I was familiar with their rules and lifestyle. If you're not familiar with gangs, a famous Hispanic movie from the early 1990s called *Blood In, Blood Out* does a good job at illustrating the gang mentality. The title refers to the concept that once you join a gang, you can never leave. You need to spill blood to get into the gang and the only way you can opt out is by dying. Dramatic, I know, but loyalty was at the core of their organization and was, perhaps, the quality the gangs valued most in their members. My exposure to gang culture went beyond the movies; growing up in San Antonio, I witnessed it firsthand.

The gangs in my area had cool names like the Kings or the Lench Mob, some of which were funny when you knew the story behind them. For example, in Hispanic culture, Lench is a nickname for Lorenzo, and even as early as elementary school, the other kids would joke that I was in the Lench Mob. There was another gang in my area that called themselves the Olmos Boys. Olmos was the name of a street near my house, but the gang didn't live on Olmos; they lived on Hermosa Drive. However, *hermosa* means "beautiful" in Spanish, and no gang wants to be known as the Beautiful Boys.

Funny names aside, the gangs in my area were intense, especially when it came to their initiation rituals. Whenever a new recruit joined a gang, the whole gang would huddle around and beat the piss out of the new member for approximately thirty seconds. Thirty seconds doesn't sound like a long time, but it's an eternity when you're getting kicked in the teeth by twelve guys in Red Wings. It was a brutal practice, but that's how new members were accepted into the gang. In the same way fraternities have hazing rituals, an initiation beat-down was how the gang established a common experience—every member had been through the same unpleasant event, and once you'd gone through it, you were a part of the group.

I saw my peers get recruited into gangs as early as middle school, when I attended the first magnet school in a rough district. Psychologically, it was a strange place to be as a young adult—the projects bordered the schoolyard, and you could see the county jail from my Latin class. Kids would bus in from all over the city to attend the school because it had the first multilingual program, and the student body was an interesting mix of kids who'd been accepted into the program and kids from the housing projects nearby.

The students tended to divide themselves into two social

groups—the "smart" out-of-district students and the local regulars—but both were susceptible to gang involvement. There were the NDs, the Junior Mexican Mafia of Texas, and the Studs of Tafolla, among others. Students needed to join a gang to avoid being targeted and bullied, but my friends and I weren't exactly gang material. We were the punk rock, grunge crew who wore flannel shirts and listened to the Ramones, Pearl Jam, and Soundgarden. We were different, which made us the common enemy of all the gangs. The only thing that saved us was one of our members, a six-foot-three, three-hundred-pound Mexican kid named Robert, aka Big Mac.

My crew had Big Mac as a bodyguard to protect us from any serious harm, and we fought back against the other gangs by ridiculing them relentlessly. We decided to pick a name for our crew that mocked the gangs and began calling ourselves the Kool Flannel Club, or KFC. The satire went right over the heads of the gang members, but the point is that we were a legit group, and we were loyal to each other. Loyalty was something that was forced on me out of necessity, for defense, but I learned at this young age that everyone needs a group.

One thing that many people don't talk about is the inevitability of joining a posse once you enter the workforce. Everyone experiences posses in high school. They're the mean girls who don't let other people sit with them at lunch, the punk rockers who smoke under the bleachers, and the jocks who stuff the nerds in lockers. You'll see the same trends in the office: the sales people have a posse, the managers have a posse, the IT people have a posse, and so on.

Here's the good news: unlike high school cliques, corporate posses won't beat you up when you join. What does happen is you start self-selecting people who share something in common with you. People tend to develop loyalty to their corporate posse, and when someone from your posse goes to a new company, they can take you with them. Posses of people who used to work together were some of the first I noticed in the workplace, and something I experienced personally at Rackspace.

When my friend James Brehm started working at Rackspace, he convinced me to leave Gateway and join him there. Then we brought over a guy named Freddie Garcia, and one named Greg Rodriguez, and then Dax Moreno, Luke Owen, Bobby Boughton, and Scott White. It wasn't long until we had a whole corporate posse made up of ex-Gateway employees. Later, the same thing happened when a large group of Dell employees joined the company.

When you start a new job, you're going to join someone's posse, and you need to choose wisely. Their networks become your networks, and yours becomes theirs. These are people who will be in your career network forever. Just remember, loyalty is the glue that holds networks together and the catalyst that can open doors. In short, whether in the schoolyard or the boardroom, loyalty is necessary for success.

LOYALTY THAT RUNS DEEP

School taught me loyalty out of necessity, but I learned about loyalty out of love from my family. My father has always been a fiercely loyal Dallas Cowboys fan, and there was a famous game between the Cowboys and 49ers one year in which Joe Montana threw a touchdown pass known as "The Catch" to win the game for the 'Niners. I was too young to remember, but my brother Danny said a part of our father died that day. He was never the same after that loss, and it was because of how deep his loyalty to the Dallas Cowboys ran. Loyalty is about committing yourself to a person, team, or ideal so fully, it becomes a part of you.

I found that working for a winning team like H-E-B inspired loyalty, but I didn't truly internalize the concept of loyalty until I learned how to fish. Danny is an avid fisherman and introduced me to the sport, although I've never mastered it as well as him, and I still need a hand tying my line knots. To this day, we visit Bob Hall Pier every November, usually at midnight on a Monday when no one else is around. We pay our two dollars per fishing pole to get onto the pier and walk out five hundred yards into the ocean. Then, we fish.

The pier has always been a magical place. Over the years, my brother and I have had trips where we've come home empty-handed, and others reminiscent of Ernest Hemingway's *Old Man and the Sea*, where we would battle the bull reds all night. My go-to tactic has always been using fish heads for bait, but one day, Danny and I brought Pops fishing with us, and I changed my strategy. I tried using the meaty body of the fish but had no luck. I switched to using squid and still couldn't get any bites. Finally, after hours of being unsuccessful, I went back to my old standard of fish heads.

Within minutes, I hooked a perch. I felt so proud and turned to my father to tell him that switching back to fish heads worked. He gave me the kind of huge grin only a father can give and said something that left a profound impact on me, "Lench, you have to dance with the one who brought you." Fish heads were what worked, and they were a strategy worth keeping.

It was such a simple and accurate concept about loyalty that applied to both personal and professional aspects of life. For example, my friend Dax Moreno is the person who brought me to Gateway. In doing so, he paid me a favor, and the idea of betraying his trust by being disloyal was unthinkable. The same principle applied when James Brehm vouched for me at Rackspace. That day, he earned my undying allegiance.

LOYALTY IS WORTH ITS WEIGHT IN GOLD

Like hard work and a good reputation, loyalty is a form of currency. In my opinion, it's the most valuable form of social currency and should be treated like a precious gem. Giving your loyalty to someone is a special gift. Like a rare gem, it should last forever. Loyalty isn't something to be granted lightly or given to people who are undeserving, and you owe it to yourself to be selective.

Dax was the first person I met who guarded his loyalty with the ferocity of a junkyard dog. He was skeptical of people and had assigned a different currency value to his loyalty than I had, which made me realize I needed to raise my price. I hadn't realized I'd lowered the value of my loyalty to the point where I was kind of a loyalty floozy. Anyone who was nice to me could earn my loyalty, but you only have so much loyalty to give. Knowing I had Dax's hard-earned loyalty made me value our friendship all the more because I knew it was rare.

My advice to you is to carefully consider the cost of your loyalty. What does someone need to do to earn it? Once you have that answer, don't compromise, but also be sure to honor your loyalty once it's earned. To the people who are worthy, your loyalty should last forever.

The above advice is, of course, void if someone no longer deserves your loyalty. Similar to veto power and choosing who earns a spot on your personal board of directors, nobody can make decisions about loyalty for you. It's one of the few things in life you have complete control over, which makes it one of the most powerful currencies in your pocket. You can wake up tomorrow and say you're not going to be loyal to your family anymore, and that's your decision. My family has my undying loyalty, but some families aren't worthy. I hope you won't ever have to make the decision to sever loyalties with someone, but if you do, remember it's your choice to make.

IT TAKES TWO TO DANCE

When you dance with the one who brought you, they'll dance back. You'll see throughout your career, time and time again, that people reward those who have been loyal to them. When Graham Weston offered me my job at the 80/20 Foundation, I couldn't understand the reasoning behind his decision. At the time, I had worked at Rackspace for a decade and had recently left to go to a startup. I remember calling Dax and explaining my confusion—why would Graham select me to be the face of his private foundation?

Dax replied, "I don't know if you realize this, but you've been interviewing for this job for the past ten years." Suddenly, it became clear to me that one of the qualities Graham valued most in his employees was loyalty. For over ten years, I had unknowingly proven that I was loyal to him, loyal to the mission, and loyal to the company. Not only was I loyal, but I followed through on that loyalty. Loyalty landed me a job I didn't even know I was applying for, and that's the career-changing power of dancing with the one who brought you.

As you get older, more things in life tend to depend on loyalty. Graham first offered me the job at the 80/20 Foundation and later hired me at Geekdom, which is one of the largest coworking spaces in Texas. I remember sitting in my hundredth meeting with people who were asking Graham for funding. I wondered how he handled the constant stream of demands, but over time, I realized he valued the currency of loyalty over the currency of money, and the one had to precede the other.

I shared Graham's values regarding loyalty and put them into practice. When I received a job offer from a prominent tech company, which I learned through personal channels would pay me nearly double my salary at the time, I had to decline. I needed to weigh the intangibles: Graham gave me an opportunity that no one else would and access to people that no one else could. The offering executive became quite angry when I told him, "No, thank you." He represented a huge tech company that anybody would want to work for, and I don't think he was used to people turning him down. I explained that Graham had given me so much and that I wasn't willing to betray him. A higher paycheck simply wasn't worth the loss of long-term, well-earned loyalty to me.

Money is one of the few things I don't consider—especially in the early years of your career—a good variable when faced with a crisis of loyalty. The exception is if you need the extra income to solve a timely issue, like keeping your parents from losing their house. If you don't need the money for an emergency, hurting your reputation by job hopping isn't worth a minor raise. Once you get branded as a job hopper, you'll have a much harder time getting hired by companies that offer the chance for personal development and skills acquisition, which will have far greater ramifications than a little extra money in the long run.

CATEGORIZING LOYALTY FROM ZERO TO TEN

While working at Rackspace, I learned about a methodology called Net Promoter Score, or NPS. It's a concept developed by Fred Reichheld meant to test customer loyalty with a brief survey. The question it asks is this: "Would you recommend this product, person, or company to a friend or colleague?"

Answers are ranked on a scale of zero to ten. A rating of six or less is referred to as a detractor—these are the people sharing a bad experience who will negatively impact a company or person's reputation. A rating of seven or eight is passive and represents a lack of loyalty—as soon as they're presented with a better offer, passive people will abandon your company. A rating of nine or ten means the person is a promoter. These are the ideal customers—people who are loyal to your brand and go out of their way to share their enthusiasm with others. In effect, they're unpaid salespeople.

The second question the NPS asks, which produces the most useful information, is simply, "Why?" Everyone has reasons for loving or hating the things they feel strongly about, and having that insight can be invaluable when you need to make changes. The goal of any company is to create loyal customers who will promote their brand, but the goal for people should be the same. Are there people in your life who will enthusiastically advocate on your behalf? What about detractors? Who are you willing to promote? Answer those questions, and be damn sure you know the "why" behind them.

DON'T BE SEDUCED BY GREENER GRASS

As a young adult still new to the workforce, I was eager to pledge my allegiance and loyalty to someone worthy. When H-E-B Number Five promoted me to the produce department and I joined their tight-knit team, I found my opportunity. I finally felt like I had a place to invest my loyalty, and I took great pride in supporting my department. Soon after, I realized there will always be something that tests your loyalty.

My father often warned my siblings and me about the false allure of other opportunities. If I came home complaining about my boss, he would sit me down and say, "Lench, the grass is always greener on the other side." The subtext he communicated was to not give up your loyalty just yet, because everywhere you go has bad managers. Everywhere has bad customers. Everywhere has lazy coworkers who will drive you crazy. However, you won't see those problems from the outside, which makes other opportunities seem superior to the one you're experiencing. Be loyal to the people who already helped you out and gave you an opportunity.

Working at a grocery store, it's easy to get swept up by the greener-grass myth, because when you make an hourly wage, tiny issues tend to matter more than they should. The partners at H-E-B Number Five would often talk about other stores, especially ones on the affluent side of town. Little rumors would turn into urban legends, and I'd hear comments like, "At Number Twenty-Four, they pay everyone more than us," or, "The girls at Number Twenty-Four all look like models and will go out with you if you ask them." The way my coworkers spoke about it, you'd think H-E-B Number Twenty-Four was the Shangri-la of San Antonio grocery stores—but it wasn't. When you saw through the ridiculous stories, it became apparent that every workplace had the same kind of problems. There is no utopia.

I didn't experience the grass-is-always-greener phenomenon firsthand until after my promotion to the produce department at H-E-B Number Five. It happened when I worked extra shifts at the Thousand Oaks and Jones Maltsberger

H-E-B on the nice side of town, where I picked up extra shifts. A sharply dressed, older Hispanic man named Eddie ran the produce department at Thousand Oaks. His impeccable presentation always caught me off guard, considering part of the job was to pick out rotten vegetables and throw them in the trash. I always ended up with a dirty apron, but every shift, Eddie had on an ironed, freshly starched H-E-B shirt, dress slacks, nice shoes, and fragrant Tres Flores hair grease.

Eddie worked as hard or harder than anyone else, but he always made sure he looked presentable. He liked working with me, and I wanted to impress him because he, in turn, was so impressive. Eddie had built a loyal crew and had a nice young guy, who was his second-in-command, ready to take over the produce department when Eddie retired. Three other young guys were Eddie's go-to soldiers; like a commanding general, when he spoke, they listened. The five of them worked like a well-disciplined regiment, manning the produce department with swift efficiency.

I'll never forget the day they asked me to join their team. I was working an early-morning shift when the team did something I'd never seen them do before—they took a break to get tacos. Eddie took off his apron and asked me to join them. I felt honored that a man who was, essentially, the Vito Corleone of this neighborhood store had invited me, and I walked a little taller than usual. Eddie told me to get whatever I wanted because he was buying. I ordered my bacon and egg tacos and sat down at a nearby picnic bench. I assumed we were just taking a break to get some food and would then return to work, but Eddie looked at me and said, "Lorenzo, we want to talk to you."

He told me I had impressed the team with my work ethic, and they wanted me to leave H-E-B Number Five to work at their store full time. The offer shocked me so much, I froze midbite. I had just encountered my first crisis of loyalty. I looked up to Eddie and his team, respected them, and enjoyed working with them, but could I betray Number Five? I had a queasy, sinking feeling in my gut as I tried to figure out how I'd gotten myself into that situation. It had never been my intention to earn the loyalty of another team. All I'd wanted to do was work a few extra hours per week.

Thankfully, Eddie didn't push his offer. If he'd been an aggressive salesperson, he would've closed the deal right then. I would've been too afraid to say no, but I think he was confident enough that he didn't feel the need to be overly persuasive. He told me to think about the offer, and then he let me off the hook for the day. I'm sure he could see the terror in my eyes. We finished eating our tacos and went back to work like normal, but when I got home that night, I still had a dilemma of loyalty to resolve.

I did the one thing I would recommend to anyone facing a hard decision: I consulted my board of directors. My family helped me put the choice into perspective and realize my loyalty was firmly with Number Five. The Thousand Oaks team had nothing to offer me I couldn't get at my home store, and I loved my regular team. My managers and coworkers had invested a lot of time and energy into training me. It didn't feel right to brush them off. The thought of doing so brought on enough guilt and anxiety to confirm my decision.

I called Eddie and thanked him for the offer. I said, while I was humbled that he wanted me to join his team, Number Five had been good to me and I felt like I owed it to them to stay. Eddie graciously accepted my decline and left the door open on the offer in the event I decided to transfer to Thousand Oaks in the future. Alas, that was never meant to be. I stopped picking up extra hours at Thousand Oaks because I felt ashamed by my crisis of loyalty, as though I had come close to committing career infidelity. I decided right then and there that I was loyal to my team at Number Five. It would take nothing less than a big opportunity to convince me to leave.

My father was right about the grass always being greener. Sometimes, you need to be loyal. The right time to leave is when you find an opportunity that will teach you new skills, ones you can't acquire at your current place of employment. Weigh the pros and cons of what you're leaving versus what you're gaining on a case-by-case basis, but in general, you'll find that dancing with the one who brought you pays off in the long run.

WHY LOYALTY IS IMPORTANT

Every time you leave a job to go somewhere new, you need to start from scratch. The people who know and appreciate you won't be at your new workplace, so you'll need to build those important connections from the ground up. Starting from scratch has some upsides, for example, the opportunity to expand your network, but many of the pluses are short-term benefits. If you leave one store because another is offering you a three-dollar-per-hour raise, that's not a good enough reason. You need to play the long game, and the results of loyalty as a strategy grow over time.

I'm not suggesting that you be reckless. If there are obvious signs that a company is going downhill, it might make sense to find a new role in a more stable environment. If you're not getting mentorship or acquiring skills at your current job, look elsewhere. If you're loyal to a person rather than a company, it's entirely acceptable to defect with them to a new company. Lacking red flags, staying loyal and putting in time at a single company is the better path. No one has ever decided not to hire an applicant because they're too loyal—it's always a good quality and social currency to possess.

Loyalty is the difference between a transactional relationship and a real relationship. I've lived in multiple big cities, which are notorious for their transactional relationships. Frequently, the meetings I attended in London and New York boiled down to three interactions. My colleagues and I would exchange introductions, say what we needed from the other person, and figure out an exchange that would allow us to move on with our business. It's a transaction focused solely on resolving a problem in the most straightforward, pragmatic way with no loyalty involved.

In San Antonio and many other small cities, businesses are built on real relationships. Many times, I've seen someone who isn't used to building these types of professional relationships flounder and fail because a necessary part of the process is telling people your story. It's about getting to know business contacts and building trust. No one is allowed to skip this process, because it's the expected way to show someone that you intend to invest time in them. Your priority isn't quickly closing a deal, it's about building a working relationship. To succeed in business, you need to be aware of what level of loyalty is expected.

NO MAN IS AN ISLAND

"Nothing brings together a team like a common enemy."

—KHALED SAFFOURI

There is a big lie that gets fed to people when they join the workforce. Perhaps the Internet makes it worse, or it's Hollywood's fault. Regardless of how it's spread, the lie is this: behind every epically successful business, one person did it all. Steve Jobs changed the world with Apple. Bill Gates revolutionized computers with Microsoft. Mark Zuckerberg is the genius behind Facebook.

I don't mean to take away from these individuals' contributions, but to say they accomplished so much without help is a flat-out myth. One thing I've learned in my career is that there's a difference between individual contributors and people that get made into superheroes. Extraordinary people do extraordinary things, but they don't do it alone. Without his brother Roy Disney, Walt Disney would have been a bankrupt ideator. He needed his brother, but history only tells us of the genius that was Walt Disney.

This principle came to life for me when Graham Weston recommended I read a book titled *Power of 2* by Rodd Wagner and Gale Muller, PhD. In this book, they explore the assertion that most game-changing work, whether in sports, corporate America, or technology, was performed by teams. Time and time again, they found multiple minds behind the most exciting innovations.

If you're at a company that has a superhero figure, understand that behind the curtain, there's a team. This relates to you as a young professional in that you shouldn't spend all your time trying to be the superhero. You want to be a remarkable, high-performing contributor, which may, incidentally, put you in the spotlight as an added benefit.

For example, if you're a rock-star salesperson and exceed your goal, you'll get noticed—but you're still part of a team. Your hard work elevates the status of the entire team, which your coworkers will appreciate and respect. If someone says,

"Lorenzo built a billion-dollar company," that's an example of one person getting credit for the work of several high-performing contributors, which can breed resentment from snubbed teammates. You need to think about the success of your whole team, rather than only looking out for yourself, because no one person can do it all.

LESSONS IN TEAMWORK

The first place I learned about teamwork was working in the H-E-B produce department. I was so proud of my promotion that I walked in on that first day with a swagger in my step. I remember strolling past the cash registers with my apron hanging casually over my shoulder and my new Red Wing boots on, and looking down on all of the cashiers and baggers. The success had gone to my head, but when I met my new team, it was a sobering moment.

My new teammates were such high performers that I realized almost immediately that I needed to up my game to avoid dragging them down. The first guy on the team was named Lalo. He always wore the coolest tennis shoes and a high-and-tight haircut because he was in the Army Reserves. He could make jokes, but he busted his butt and was disciplined above all else. My second teammate was a quiet, older Hispanic man named Alberto. Alberto hadn't fully mastered English, but he had kind eyes and, like Eddie from the store across town, was always professional.

My third teammate was a huge guy named J.J. who was a beast of burden on the job. We'd have weightlifting competitions in the back of the produce department, and I have a vivid memory of J.J. curling two sacks of potatoes that would've taken my entire body to move. My fourth teammate was a tall, skinny guy named Richard, the assistant manager. He was the first Hispanic guy I'd ever met who looked Anglo, but his Spanish was so fluent you'd think he'd been born in Mexico. My last teammate was our manager, Dave. Dave introduced me to corporate politics by telling me everything we needed to do to keep our department successful and safe.

While I was part of this high-performing team, I learned all about the little rituals and habits that made us work so well together. There are four rules that can apply to any workplace: make the mundane fun, have a shared language, engage in nicknamification, and maintain a diverse team.

MAKE THE MUNDANE FUN

To this day, working on the produce team at Number Five was both the hardest I've ever worked and the most fun. There was a direct correlation between the two in that the fun we had was a direct result of our hard work. We worked so hard that the pressure would build up and we'd need to release it as fun. Most memorable were the times when we worked in pairs to cull the bad fruits and vegetables. We'd go from display to display switching out the produce, and every time a catchy song came on the radio, Richard and I would look at each other. Then, he'd start singing in the most womanly voice I've ever heard.

We'd sing Whitney Houston's "I Wanna Dance with Somebody" together like two little girls. Then, we'd get back to work and put our heads down, breaking apart nine-foot pallets of produce until lunchtime, when our shift ended. Singing was a release valve that balanced out the stress of our hard work. It made the work enjoyable, and the small pleasure of being able to sing because we were in the back of the store, unlike the cashiers, felt like a job perk. Find ways to have fun at work, and your whole team will be much happier.

HAVE A SHARED LANGUAGE

I talked about shared language earlier in the book, but I want to revisit it through the lens of relying on a team. In the same way gangs can have secret signs, workplaces can have a shared language. At Rackspace, it was the Strengths Finder personality test. Every employee had to take the test, which identifies your top strengths. The results were our shared language. People talked about their strengths, and most people had them posted on their desk or office badge. Most importantly, Strengths Finder gave us the ability to walk up to any fellow employee and start a conversation.

At H-E-B, the company referred to employees as partners, but the employees had their own shared language as well. Something unique to my store, Number Five, was the Spanish word *eso*. Literally translated, it means "that," but we used it as a nonsense word that could be applied to anything and anyone. Everyone in the store knew it, from the partners in the back to the stockers, the meat cutters, and the produce department.

As an example of a regular interaction at Number Five, I walked into the store one morning and Jesse, the overnight general manager who was finishing an all-night shift stocking the cereal aisle, saw me and said, "Eso! What's up Lorenzo?"

I replied, "What's up, Jesse? Eso," and went about my business.

Another time, I was breaking down produce pallets at four in the morning when another employee came around the corner with a buffing machine. All I knew about him was that he'd recently been released from prison and was putting in his transitional work time. He came through the produce department with his buffer, and we locked eyes. He only said one word: "Eso."

Of course, I said "Eso" back.

The word was everywhere. You'd be stocking groceries in

complete silence when one of the other stockers would yell, "Eso!"

Immediately, an echo would come: "Eso."

You'd say, "Eso, tell me about your date last night."

"Oh man, it was awesome. We're going out again this weekend."

"Eso."

Eso was such a weird phenomenon, but it was our store's common language. It was the word we said before or after anything else, a word we used to fill in the blanks. A word that meant, "You're part of the gang."

ENGAGE IN NICKNAMIFICATION

Nicknamification is an important subrule of shared language. Nicknames are unique to each individual and a term of endearment that says, "I know a part of your personality a little better than other people, and here's the nickname to prove it." I've never offended a coworker by using a nickname, although it's certainly possible, but I've seen many times when nicknames have brought a team closer.

Nicknames were a critical part of the culture at Rackspace.

The day I started at Rackspace, there was another new employee named Khaled Saffouri, whom I now consider a member of my personal board of directors. Khaled called me Eso because of my stories, and over the years, he became the most vocal advocate of nicknamification at the whole company. Most of the nicknames I heard at Rackspace were either created by Khaled or benefitted from his input.

He once explained why nicknames are so important in a company culture. He told me, "A nickname says that I value your friendship more than I value you as a coworker." What is so impressive about this statement is that Khaled was a VP of Sales and had to fire hundreds of people throughout his career. In many cases, those people were his friends who had a Khaled-created nickname. However, what he will tell you is that the nickname-level of intimacy allowed him to genuinely tell them that he had their best interests in mind. It allowed him to say, "You know I care about you, but Rackspace is just not the best place for you. Let me help find the right place for you."

Though Khaled was much more prolific, I can claim responsibility for a few Rackspace nicknames. One day in conversation with a coworker, I tried to describe Khaled. My guy crush on him manifested in a spontaneous nickname when I said, "He's the L.B.P. The Lebanese Brad Pitt." The nickname stuck and, suddenly, everyone in the sales department referred to Khaled as the L.B.P.

I also worked with an account manager named Vladimir Mata, who was one of the most effective salespeople I'd ever met. He gave me the nickname of Locon, which was his slang, hybrid way of saying "crazy guy." I loved the nickname so much, I assigned it back to him. For the next fifteen years, we referred to each other exclusively as Locon. When we were on the phone with a customer who was screaming at us, Locon was our little way of saying we had each other's back.

My last example is a coworker at Rackspace named Matt Emerson. Matt was a Linux engineer who wore glasses and had a million-dollar smile. He was shy, but he was also the nicest guy in the office and laughed at all my jokes. Thus, he could do no wrong in my book. I referred to Matt one day in conversation and wanted to compliment him. Out of nowhere, a nickname came to me: Sexy E. Emerson. Everyone who adored Matt as much as I did, which included a lot of people because he was such a thoughtful, helpful guy, started calling him Sexy E. From then on, Matt always giggled and turned bright red when someone called him Sexy E., and we loved him for it.

In Matt's case, the neat result of nicknamification is it forced him to be more social—usually, he kept to himself and didn't interject into other people's conversations—but the nickname introduced an intimacy to the team that brought us all closer. Every team doesn't need to use nicknames, but when you see nicknames being used, it's usually the output of a great team.

MAINTAIN A DIVERSE TEAM

I touched on this before, but it's important enough to warrant repeating: you need diversity on your team. If you're working with people who look just like you, talk like you, and think like you, run the other direction. Tina Fey's book *Bossypants* includes a good discussion on diversity and why it's critical to effective teams. She describes how Lorne Michaels, the executive producer of *Saturday Night Live*, has a methodology for assembling his teams of writers and comedians.

Most notably, if a team has too much of the same comedic style, the jokes fall flat. For example, too many Tina Feys with a hustling style of comedy would result in a show that was all low-brow fart jokes. On the other hand, if all you had were Harvard graduates like Conan O'Brien, you'd only get high-brow jokes about eating lobster in Martha's Vineyard. Put these two opposing forces together on a team, and now you have magic. It is the collision of these radically different worldviews that makes for interesting outcomes.

At Rackspace, diversity allowed us to provide above-average customer service because we were able to direct customers to the person most qualified to deal with their problem. Every company has employees with different specializations, but what made a difference at Rackspace was the positioning. We put a billing person next to an account manager, next to a salesperson, next to an engineer—and we were a single team. If someone came in with a technical problem, we could quickly direct them to the right person rather than having to coordinate between departments. Mixing up teams changed the business for the better.

HOW YOU FIT INTO A TEAM

Your first job when you join a new team should be figuring out what you can bring to the table. Do you have any special skills? What's not being done on the team that you can help with? If you already know what unique skills you have, you're ahead of the curve. You can figure out very quickly how you fit into the team. If you don't know your place, the best way to find out is to take on an apprentice role. Swallow your pride and tell your teammates that you're there to learn. It's a gesture that shows you know you're not an island while also subtly acknowledging that your more senior teammates know more than you.

When I joined Rackspace, I realized I didn't know what servers were or how the Internet really worked. Immediately after, I realized everyone else could tell I didn't know, too. I had a decision to make. I could either deny that I knew nothing and potentially make a huge mistake while helping a customer, or I could ask my teammates for help when I needed it. In truth, it wasn't much of a choice—there is only one right answer.

One time, an angry customer called because someone

hacked their Microsoft server. I knew I couldn't handle the problem on my own, so I went to Adam, a Windows engineer, for help. Now, this was a tricky situation because I needed him to know that if he said no, I was helpless. I wasn't pretending to be clueless so I could pass my job off onto him; I genuinely needed his expertise. I told him, "Adam, you know a lot about Windows, and I know nothing about it, but I have an angry customer on my hands. If you could get on the phone with this customer, I'll handle all the backend stuff and issue the credit. But man, I would really love your help on the Windows issues."

I had no other option but to ask for Adam's help, and it worked out for me because I positioned myself as an apprentice. I conveyed to the team, "I'm here to learn. What do you need me to do?" If you need to ask your teammates for help—which you will at some point—counterbalance it by offering to help whenever you can, even if it's just grabbing coffee.

Assess your skills and figure out how you can help. Do you know how to enter data? Can you answer phones? Is there anything else you can help with while your coworker is helping you? Find ways to make yourself useful, and over time, you'll earn the right to be a peer on equal footing.

CULLING AND SHRINK

When I worked at the grocery store, part of my job was to cull the fruits and vegetables using one of two methods. The first involved removing the rotten produce, then moving the older—but still sellable—produce to the front of the display, and then placing the fresh items in the back. The second method involved removing the older produce, putting the new items on the bottom of the display, and then restacking the older fruits and vegetables on top.

The culling strategies are the reason you'll see little old ladies reaching for the back of the stack—they're savvy to our methods and know where to find the freshest produce. When you work in produce, little old ladies are your arch nemeses, engaged in an ongoing battle in which you try to foil their efforts. They want the new fruit, but if you let produce sit on the shelf for too long, it goes bad.

Usually culling wasn't a problem, but once a year, H-E-B would get a shipment of plumcots, which are hybrid plum-apricots. The first time I opened a case, I had no idea what the strange fruits were. We only received three boxes, which was also odd, as our normal produce orders were much larger. Part of my job was to test the produce and put a sticker on the display to confirm it was fresh. When I tried the plumcot, it was the most magical piece of fruit I had ever eaten. Nobody ever bought the plumcots, and they would often go bad, so I made the somewhat-unethical decision to leave a few in the back room for me to eat.

I was committing what's known in the produce department as shrink, which refers to any theft or damaging of goods. Shrink is the Darth Vader of the grocery world—enemy number one—and it was the employees' job to mitigate it as much as possible. Admittedly, I failed in my duty when it came to the plumcots, but I reasoned that an exception could be made because they were spoiling anyway.

Shrink can happen in several ways. If you drop a carton of milk on the floor and it spills everywhere, that counts as shrink, as does a cashier slipping a candy bar in their pocket on the way out the door. Shrink occurred frequently in the grocery store, but I encountered it in other workplaces as well.

When I manned the Gateway kiosk at OfficeMax, I worked beside a stocker named Rene. One day, Rene was pushing a cart through the store when he stopped at my kiosk. As cool as Fonzie, he looked at me and said, "Hey, I'll sell this to you for half-off." He shifted his gaze downward. I followed his line of sight and, sitting in the cart, was a single PalmPilot—which was the precursor to the iPad for us old people.

Rene had been slowly stealing inventory, one piece at a time. Then, when he helped customers with the PalmPilots, he'd wait until he had built a rapport before telling the customer that he owned a device himself and would sell it for half price. He was stealing inventory and selling it back to the customers, which I thought was pretty gutsy. In the hood, we called this the five-finger discount. I didn't approve of him committing shrink, but I wasn't a rat. In hindsight, I probably should've blown the whistle, but Rene was a potentially dangerous guy, and it wasn't a battle I wanted to fight.

An instance of shrink that bothered me even more than Rene's sticky PalmPilot fingers took place at H-E-B. Once a year, we'd enter a season of produce that was glorious for the customers and absolutely dreaded by the produce employees, including me: pistachio season. I hated pistachio season with a passion, more than I hated rotten tomatoes or the Shania Twain song H-E-B played over the intercom ten times a day.

When pistachio season was in full swing, we'd order the nuts by the ton, and every day the pistachios were out, I'd see rampant shrink take place right before my eyes. Shrink happened on such a massive scale, there was no way to stop it—it was shrinkapalooza. For that one season, every customer at Number Five thought it was acceptable to commit theft. They'd take pistachios and eat them for free, then leave the shells everywhere throughout the store.

Seeing customers steal without remorse made me hate

humanity for that one season. I'd say to myself, "I can't believe these people; they're a bunch of thieves. Did their parents not raise them right? Do they have no respect for law and order?" What offended me the most was that they didn't even have the decency to hide what they were doing. People would openly eat the stolen pistachios and toss the shells wherever they pleased. If I was cleaning behind the boxes of cereal, I'd find pistachio shells. Relocating the peanut butter and jelly section? Pistachio shells. Pistachio shells everywhere.

As a young professional, you should be aware that there's shrink at all levels. Shrink isn't limited to PalmPilots and pistachios, but occurs at every company and on every team, and even on a personal level. My advice is to take a good, hard look at the people in your life. Are there people damaging your self-esteem? Are they stealing your ideas? Are they wasting your time? You can lose money, talent, time, and reputation, and it all falls under the category of shrink.

Returning to my original story, my decision to commit shrink of the plumcots stemmed from the fact that the fruit sat on the shelf too long. The parallel I want to draw is that, sometimes, you have to cull people. There will come a time when someone on your team is too old—not in age, but in mentality. They won't be open to new ideas and methodologies, and you'll need to cull them from your group. Even more difficult is when you have to cull friends. If you have a friend who has stopped advancing or is committing shrink against you, you need to cull them or they'll hold you back.

Harder still is when you need to cull someone from your board of directors. Sometimes, the cause is as innocuous as losing touch with a person. There's nothing wrong with that happening, but you need to make a decision to remove that person from your board for a while. Like produce, friendships, ideas, and employees will go bad if you let them sit too long.

THE UNSPOKEN RULES OF SOCIAL AGREEMENTS

In the workplace, you're expected to adhere to certain unspoken social agreements. These agreements, while not always explicitly defined, are important to follow because they allow everyone to conduct business on the same page. My thinking on this topic changed when I read a book called *Predictably Irrational: The Hidden Forces That Shape Our Decisions* by Dan Ariely. In his book, Ariely talks about social agreements and uses the example of attending Thanksgiving at your mother-in-law's house. The scenario describes finishing dinner, pulling out your checkbook, and asking your mother-in-law how much you owe her.

If the dinner were a business transaction at a restaurant, pulling out your checkbook would be an appropriate reaction. However, dinner with your in-laws is a social engagement, and offering to pay money would be a grievous insult to the host that would likely earn you a slap to the face. Different reactions to different, but similar, scenarios are expected because we live in two worlds—one world is governed by market agreements, and the other is governed by social agreements. You never want to treat a social agreement like a market agreement or vice versa.

Every team in corporate America has its own unspoken social agreements, but they also have stated market agreements, such as how much they'll pay you, what your title is, and your responsibilities. Companies often try to hint at their social agreements in places like their core values or mission statements, but those don't always provide a clear picture. The social agreements can be much trickier to recognize and follow because they're not discussed or written down, but it's important for you to try to discern them when you join a new team. Understanding the dynamics of your team's social agreements can make or break your role at that company.

A while back, I worked at a company with two men. One was the head finance controller, and the other was his subordinate. However, they had worked together at a previous company where the roles had been the opposite. When they came to the company where I worked, their titles changed, but their relationship did not. The guy who had become the number two still bossed around the other guy, as well as everyone beneath him.

He had a whole department of billing, accounts, and receiving people who understood how the hierarchy actually worked, despite what was on paper. To follow the social agreement on that team, you needed to sell your idea to the number-two guy because he was the one calling the shots. If you didn't understand the social agreement and treated the number-one guy like the boss, you'd alienate the number-two guy and make an enemy.

The above example shows the kind of corporate politics you'll inevitably face in the workforce, and it isn't limited to white-collar jobs. When I was on the produce team at H-E-B Number Five, I quickly realized there were social agreements that dictated the chain of command. When you performed your duties, you were expected to follow that chain of command without being told. The second social agreement mandated that we have everybody's back. If someone was struggling, the social agreement said you needed to drop what you were doing and go help them. You weren't allowed to let anyone stumble on the team. It's one of the social agreements I've often seen in other workplaces, because any high-performing team knows they're only as good as their weakest member.

One of the other unspoken rules of Number Five's social agreement was that we had fun, but we worked crazy-hard. For every one minute of fun, there were ten intense minutes of hard work. As I described in a previous story, it's one of the rules that kept us sane and allowed us to release some stress. I picked up on the have-fun-work-hard social agreement fairly quickly by noticing that we never took large blocks of time dedicated to just fun. In fact, it almost never happened.

The produce team always went one hundred miles per hour, took a short break, and then picked right back up at a breakneck speed. For example, if we had to go to the front of the veggie section, we'd go in pairs while singing along to whatever song was playing on the intercom. At the same time, we'd try to race our teammates, meaning we wanted to do the task as quickly and efficiently as possible. From my perspective at the time, there was a direct correlation between singing a song and wanting to prove to my teammates that I was such a badass that I could sing while fronting the greens.

WHY YOU NEED AN ENEMY

Another unspoken rule I've witnessed at many companies is that **nothing brings a team together like a common enemy.** I use the term *enemy* loosely, because you can have playful enemies and you can have real enemies. For example, at H-E-B, our real enemy was Walmart. Teammates at Number Five would spread rumors about how Walmart was heavily financed and would drop prices on their entire grocery section just so they could undercut us and steal our customers.

Regardless of whether those particular rumors were true, Walmart was our competition and real enemy. Nothing brought our entire company together like H-E-B's chairman telling us we were going head-to-head with Walmart, and we were going to chase them out of San Antonio. My teammates and I respected and loved H-E-B, so we all said, "Hell, yeah. Sign me up."

There's also playful opposition, or what you might call "fake enemies." Fake enemies would be your in-store competition. For example, at H-E-B, the produce team took great pride in outperforming the meat market. The meat department was located right next to produce and had an entirely different type of crew. If we had been in high school instead of a grocery store, the produce guys would've been the basketball team and the meat guys would've been the football jocks.

The meat market guys looked the part of butchers and had forearms the size of my head, wore handlebar mustaches, and acted like they were big deals. They'd walk around cutting meat all day in their white suits, but I felt bad for them because, every day, they had to break down all of their equipment and clean it. H-E-B had very high cleanliness standards, so thoroughly disinfecting the machines took quite a lot of time.

The meat market was the produce team's fake enemy, and we'd always try to generate more revenue than them, provide better service, get our work done faster, and have more fun. It was playful, healthy competition. Beneath it all, there was camaraderie—when we tested the watermelon in the back of the store before putting the "Fresh" sticker on the display, we'd invite the meat guys over to partake. Still, they were the other team, which made them the enemy. Whether it's a real enemy like Walmart or a fake enemy like the meat market guys, every team needs someone to beat.

DON'T BE A REJECTED ORGAN

When you join a new team, you need to figure out its social contract. Be aware and on the lookout because you don't want to be blindsided by it—you want the team to take you in. You'll see throughout your career that once in a while someone will join your team and unknowingly break the social rules. Worse, they might be aware of the social rules, decide they're stupid, and consciously decide not to follow them.

When someone joins a team and rejects the social agreement, it's like the human body rejecting an organ transplant. I've seen this happen many times, at every level of an organization. Sometimes a leader takes over a team, automatically assumes they're the boss, and ignores the established social agreements. The result? Their team mutinies, and they have to deal with a full-on revolt. It can be difficult for your career to recover from such a hurdle, so pay attention to your team— don't wind up a rejected organ.

When I started at Rackspace, I worked on my first support team. I was twenty years old and working with other account managers who were much older than me. Our team also had several open-source Linux engineers and Microsoft engineers who were very smart. I quickly realized I needed them more than they needed me. One of the rules of our team was that we didn't offload a problem onto an engineer, because they already had way too much work. If the problem was serious enough, the social rules dictated that I had to stand up, walk over to their desk, and plead my case.

A critical part of the social agreement with the engineers was that you needed to ask nicely. You also had to admit that you needed their help and that you weren't smarter than them. As a nontechnical person, one of the worst things you could do was pretend you understood a problem when you really had no idea what was going on. Trying to fake your knowledge was a cardinal sin.

For example, if some cocky account manager walked up to an engineer and said, "I think you need to restart this customer's web services," you would've heard the entire room gasp in shock. People would whisper, "I can't believe an account manager just tried to diagnose the issue to an engineer." One-upping or talking down to an engineer was an affront to the social agreement and always came with consequences.

The response in this scenario would be the engineer turning to the cocky account manager and saying, "No, I can't help you. I'm too busy." It'd be a straight-up organ rejection, and the manager would usually be left with the issue still on their hands and an angry customer on the phone. The point of the story is that to be successful in the workplace and have the support of your team, you need to fall in line with the rules.

WHEN YOU NEED TO BREAK A SOCIAL AGREEMENT

Sometimes, there are exceptions that will require you to break a social agreement. If the social rules are unethical, you absolutely need to get out of that environment, find another job, and possibly report them. For example, if a team's social rules involve performing tricky math in the books to secure their bonus, that's a valid reason for you to buck the agreement and opt out. A team should have good social agreements, like avoiding corporate politics, trusting each other, and not talking behind each other's backs—basic agreements that allow a team to function smoothly.

Hand-in-hand with good social agreements is a foundation of common values. As an example, Rackspace has an amazing set of core values, one of which required us to focus on results first: substance over flash. There are many reasons this is a great value; chief among them is that it's obvious when someone violates it. If a sales guy had rolled up to Rackspace in a Ferrari after his first successful year, that would be flash over substance. My team at Rackspace prided itself on working on folding plastic tables, because we knew we didn't need anything fancy to get the work done. All we needed was a place to set our laptops so we could get to the support tickets and help our customers.

Rackspace's practicality tied into another of its core values, which was to provide fanatical support in everything we did. This was a value at the company level that translated to my individual team in a few specific ways: we would never tell a customer something wasn't our job, and we would always try to at least give a customer several options. Excellent support was a promise to ourselves and to our customers.

Good social agreements and team dynamics should always reflect core values, and it's your job to think about your core values. What does it take for you to work well with a team? What are your deal breakers when it comes to interacting with colleagues? Figure out how you work best and define the values that are important to you, and then find a company that shares your outlook.

POLITICS AT THE CHECKOUT STAND

One of my goals throughout my career has been to work at companies with minimal office politics. Some companies mostly avoid it, but like my dad used to say, "There is no utopia." Every company has problems (even if you can't see them immediately), and every company engages in politics to some degree. You could run a lemonade stand, and as soon as you hire your first helper, you've introduced politics to the equation. Politics are just the way the world works, so you need to understand how to deal with it in the office if you want to be a productive teammate.

The first time I encountered politics was at my first job at Handy Andy. I was naive when I started there and expected everyone to want to work as hard as me. I quickly realized that wasn't the case. There are several types of people who engage in politics, but I'm going to profile two of the most common: the brownnoser and the bureaucrat.

EVERYBODY WANTS A JOB, BUT NOT EVERYONE WANTS TO WORK

You saw the brownnoser back in elementary school—the kid who always sucked-up to the teacher—and you'll see them again in the workplace. They're the person who uses flattery to play politics and curry favor with the boss. I saw my first brownnoser at Handy Andy in an older man named Mario. Mario was old and so close to retiring that he had checked out of the job. My father once told me a phrase he'd heard from an old Southern pastor, **"Everybody wants a job, but not everyone wants to work,"** which described Mario perfectly. He wanted a paycheck but didn't want to do any work, and he'd use his relationship with our boss, Mr. Diaz, as a way to do nothing.

Mario would do anything he could to get out of helping me or anyone else on his shift. He was a bagger, so he already had the easiest job at the grocery store, but it was still too much for him. Whenever the check stands lit up during the busiest hour, I'd look around, and Mario was nowhere to be found. I'd go looking for him, and I'd often find him in the parking lot trying to round up the three shopping carts that were out there, or anything else he could do to avoid bagging.

One time, I went outside to collect baskets and saw Mario across the street buying tacos for himself and Mr. Diaz. I remember thinking, *That son of a chupacabra.* I felt furious with him, but I realized I had to focus on doing my job and not let him get to me, which was very difficult. I felt a pain that results from certain types of politics—the pain of being abandoned by a teammate. It's a pain that relates back to the social agreements I discussed in the previous section, because when you have a team social agreement that says you all support each other and someone breaks it, the trust erodes. I thought I had a teammate in Mario, and he violated the trust. Slowly but surely, my loyalty to the company started deteriorating because my boss, Mr. Diaz, didn't regulate what was happening with Mario.

Everybody else on the team hated Mario and had already organ-rejected him, but Mr. Diaz failed to see that. In doing so, he failed in his leadership responsibilities. People like Mario engage in politics for their own benefit at great expense to the rest of the team. Ultimately, the political turmoil involving Mario and Mr. Diaz was one of the main things that led me to quit at Handy Andy. If you're on a team with someone like Mario, you and your coworkers need to organ-reject them as soon as possible.

FEELINGS ARE ALWAYS MUTUAL

In office politics, you'll also see bureaucrats who hide behind processes to get what they want. You see this a lot in government jobs where the person behind the counter at the DMV, for example, will use the excuse, "Sorry, I can't help you. That's against policy." Following the rules is important, but these are the people who seem like they don't want to help you. At every job, you'll see people hiding behind the rules as an excuse to avoid work. They're not using the rules to help the customer or the company—they're using the rules to help themselves.

The first bureaucrat I met was a guy, also named Lorenzo, who worked at Handy Andy. The fact I shared a name with him was very disconcerting to me because I was named after my grandfather, Lorenzo, who was a great man and all-around cool guy. My brother Danny told me our grandfather owned a radiator shop in Laredo that only accepted cash, so he'd walk around with a big roll of bills. He'd sit my brother on his lap and pull out a couple ones, and my brother thought he was the richest guy on the planet. I have a great affinity for my name because my grandfather was such a family legend, despite the fact that he couldn't read and could only write his name.

But there I was at Handy Andy meeting my first bureaucrat, and he happened to be named Lorenzo. Almost instantly, I hated this Lorenzo because I thought he was giving us a bad name. In hating him, I learned a principle that I couldn't put a name to for many years, until Graham shared a saying from his business partner with me: **feelings are always mutual**. I hated Lorenzo for being a bureaucrat and hiding behind rules to avoid helping people, and I could tell he hated me in return.

In the workplace, understand that feelings are always mutual. If you hate me, I probably hate you. If I think you're lazy, you probably think I'm a show off. If I think you're a Billy Badass who hung the moon, you probably think I'm not half bad either. The feelings-are-mutual principle reemerged for me years later when I was working for a coworking space. I couldn't stand a guy in the space because he treated everyone poorly, including his customers and employees. One evening at the end of the workday, he and I walked to the elevator at the same time. I'll never forget how painfully awkward it was, and at that moment, Graham's face appeared like Jiminy Cricket over my shoulder and said, "Remember, feelings are always mutual."

I looked over at the other guy waiting for the elevator and realized he couldn't stand me, which was okay, because I couldn't stand him either. I walked onto that elevator with the biggest smile on my face because I knew what was actually going on between us. I didn't have to hide behind my feelings anymore. So I said, "Hey, man. What's up?" He seemed surprised I was talking to him and said the same thing back. I felt so much better in that moment because I knew the truth of our relationship and the pressure was taken off. I wasn't going to go out of my way to be a jerk to that guy, but I accepted our mutual disdain, and I'm here to tell you, after my realization, it was the most pleasant eleven-story elevator ride I've ever taken.

Feelings are always mutual, and when you think someone is a jerk for playing politics, they think you're dumb for not doing the same. You think they're a scumbag, while they think they're going to pull one over on you, but if you stay aware of what's going on, they won't succeed. Remember that every company has politics, and you won't be shocked by the unpleasant people you meet.

Now you know to expect corporate politics wherever you go, but what should you do when you find it? The best option is usually to not engage, and there are several ways you can avoid getting involved. If the politics are a serious problem, you can run the other way by leaving the company, and if you decide to stay, you can choose to not intervene.

BEWARE THE DANGERS OF GOSSIP

The choice to abstain relates back to personal boards of directors—if you're watching someone engage in politics, it doesn't do you any good to call the person out because you're not on their board of directors. You would never ask them to be on your board of directors, and they would never ask you, so why go out of your way to call them out and make an enemy? I suggest using veto power and avoid the political drama at all costs. For example, if someone starts gossiping at the office, you can tap out. Simply say to yourself, "I'm going to work hard and do my own thing," and stay uninvolved.

Gossip and rumors are variables that are always present in office politics. Personally, engaging in gossip is something I used to struggle with, partly due to my upbringing. Every year around Christmas, my family hosts an event called La Tamalada, which basically translates to Tamales Day. It's a day when my mother and sisters prepare a huge assembly line in my mother's kitchen, invite tons of people—mostly female family members—and make tamales. There are two rules to La Tamalada: the event is invite-only, and whatever you make you take home.

The event is a big deal in my family, and there have been feuds, hurt feelings, and grudges held for years over not getting invited to it. Not receiving an invitation is a huge exclusion, partly because one of the main activities at La Tamalada, aside from making tamales, is catching up, but we all know what that really means. Many times, there would be fifteen to twenty Mexican women in my mother's kitchen, with me eating all the tamales in the background. I'd hear a nonstop stream of conversations, like, "Oh, my gosh, did you hear about him? Guess what? She's pregnant and not even married! Now he's in jail and he hasn't seen his kids in four years!"

I couldn't help but get totally sucked into the gossip like an addict. Hearing these stories would make my palms sweat and my heart race because, like a good addict, I wanted to hear just a little bit more about what was going on. I share this story to make the point that I'm not one to get on my high horse and claim I've never engaged in gossip. However, I've recognized its destructive power. I want to save you the hassle of being entangled in it, because gossip can hold you back in your career.

When my family gossiped, there wasn't any genuine malicious intent behind it, but what makes gossip so bad is that regardless of intent, you can hurt someone's self-esteem and wreck their career and reputation. There's an old verse in the Bible that says, "Reckless words pierce like a sword, but the tongue of the wise brings healing." I was listening to a Presbyterian minister on my favorite podcast one day when he brought this proverb to light. He explained that the reason the verse is so powerful is because, just like if you stabbed someone in the stomach with a real sword, when you pulled the sword out, the hole would still be there. You could say you're sorry, but it wouldn't take away the hole you left.

Words operate the same way as a sword, and this is the problem with gossip and rumors. You can't take back the things you've said. If you want to write a hotheaded e-mail to your boss, sleep on it, because once you send it out into the universe, there's no taking it back. Words are incredibly powerful and often don't get the respect or attention they deserve.

The first time I witnessed the extreme effects of words was on the check stand at H-E-B. I was hired at H-E-B after attending a job fair, along with about ten other people. We all started at the same time, and there were a few awesome characters in our cohort. There was a hilarious girl named Tony and her sister Lori, who both brought the most positive energy to the team. There was a cocky guy named David who drove a Camaro and walked with a swagger, but we were buddies.

There was another guy, Billy, who was a golden-gloves boxer.

I had great respect for Billy the boxer because my grandfather was a boxer. My mom would often tell stories about how he'd get my aunts and uncles to box each other in their backyard. Messed up, I know. I found out later that Billy's real name wasn't Billy. He had a Hispanic name like Lupe, but his coach changed it to be a "better" boxing name. I thought letting his coach change his name was crazy, but Billy was a good guy. He worked hard, had earned a high school diploma, and was going to college.

One slow day, I was working the check stand and trying to embrace the principle of having fun at work. Billy was on the check stand in front of me, while David swept the floor between us. I thought I'd play a little joke to liven the place up and said, "Hey, Billy. Did you hear about David talking shit about you, bro?" What happened next happened so quickly.

Before I could say, "Just kidding," Billy spun around, looked at David, and shouted, "What the f&*# are you saying about me? You talkin' shit behind my back?"

David, who must've known I was lying, looked up at Billy and said, "Yeah, what if I am, *puto*?"

In less than ten seconds, the situation had escalated out of my control. There Billy was in the middle of checking out a customer with his temper boiling over, and I had to jump in between him and David to keep them from fighting.

I frantically told them I was only kidding. Even though they both acknowledged that I'd made it up, a feud had started. They were like two pit bulls that had been separated and didn't get to fight. I felt awful that my reckless words had created trouble on the check stand. I realized how quickly something as simple as words can escalate, especially when you provoke two alphas who have something to prove.

Just like Billy and David almost coming to fisticuffs, office gossip can escalate quickly and ruin people's careers. Even if you're not naturally inclined to participate in gossip, stay aware of the risk. One of the biggest causes of gossip, whether in the grocery store or the corporate breakroom, is boredom. At H-E-B that day, I only started the rumor because I didn't have enough to do and was bored.

One of your missions in life should be to find enough to do. There were a bunch of things I could've been doing that day instead of joking around. I could've straightened out the magazine stand and caught up on celebrity gossip while doing it instead of creating my own. I could've sprayed down my check stand or counted my till or made sure I had all my coupons. The point is that I could've done a number of other things, but I didn't want to. I chose to play a joke that almost caused a fight.

In every job, there's always more you can do—always. You'll never convince me that you've done everything there is to do. If there's a process you've done a hundred times before, you can find a way to make it better, and there are always customers who need attention. That day, I should've waved my arms and shouted that my check stand was open until I found a customer to help. My advice to you is that if you're engaging in gossip, find something to do. Don't let boredom take you down a path that leads to fighting and ruined opportunities.

THE NEGATIVE PERSONAL EFFECTS OF OFFICE POLITICS

Not only can engaging in gossip and office politics disrupt your teammates, it's also a good way to earn yourself a negative brand. No one wants to bring a person who can't govern their own mouth onto their team, and once you earn the reputation of being a gossip, it will follow you for years.

Even if you're a hard worker, being labeled a gossip could get you rejected by a good team—the brand is that corrosive. I've seen people flatline their careers because they couldn't keep their mouths shut. I nearly did it to myself when I was unhappy with a manager and wanted to let the world know. Even now, I still think I had a good reason to be angry, but it doesn't matter. All the world saw was an angry guy who didn't know how to control his mouth.

I had to work many years to get my reputation back, and I'm

here to tell you that it isn't worth it. Running your mouth can also affect you on a personal level by isolating your board members. A great friend of mine and board member was at a company where he wasn't happy. I had another friend who knew someone who also wasn't happy at the same company, and I made the mistake of telling friend number two about friend number one's unhappiness. Word got back to the owner of the company, and he called out friend number one, which led to friend number one leaving that job.

I felt absolutely horrible that I had, through my words, inadvertently hurt my friend. He's a gracious board member of mine, so he forgave me, but at the time, I wanted to crawl under a rock and live there. Even when you have good intentions, you can isolate your mentors and board members with careless words. Guard your thoughts, and if in doubt, don't say anything.

THE PRICE OF POLITICS

People will use politics to climb the food chain and there's no stopping them, but one thing I've noticed is that karma always catches up with them. When we think about karma, we think about good versus evil—the light and dark sides of the Force. The dark side of the Force is powerful, and the people who use it will quickly climb the corporate ladder. They'll make it to the top and get a lot of money, but **the bill comes due**. Their grasp for power will, inevitably, lead to them being isolated and rejected. People won't want to work with them, because they'll have earned a bad brand, and the politics will backfire.

If you feel discouraged by seeing someone at your company ascend the ladder by stepping over other people, remember that the bill always comes due. You can't stop them, but you can vote with your reputation. When someone asks if you would work for that person, you can say no. You can refuse to refer them or their company. In the corporate world, karma means bad people take their brand with them.

SECTION III

LIVING IN THE REAL WORLD

Have a Servant's Heart

———

"The ability to change someone's day is a superpower."

—L.G. III

When I started at Rackspace, I realized everyone has customers. Whether you're in administration, sales, or support, there's always a customer to serve, and one of the best ways to ensure job security is to have a role that's close to customer service. The last people to get laid off are people who serve customers directly, but everyone serves in some way.

When people think about customers, they usually think of external customers—for example, a cashier serving a customer who comes in to buy a pack of gum—but often, your customers are internal. As an account manager, I was a customer to the billing department, and the billing department was a customer to the software engineers who wrote their software, and so on. The salespeople were customers of mine. My point is that nobody gets out of customer service, and the key to approaching customers is to have a servant's heart.

Having a servant's heart doesn't mean letting customers treat you poorly. You should never be yelled at or verbally abused, which are things I put up with early in my career. Life is too short for that, but you should always have a servant's heart to help you avoid an abusive situation in the first place. Nothing upsets a customer more than waiting to get served, especially if they see the worker acting like they don't care or like their job's an inconvenience. When someone's been waiting in line for an hour but sees the person helping them working hard, they're ten times more likely to cut the worker some slack.

Having a servant's heart means wanting to help people, and it's one of the few superpowers you can deploy that no one can give you—it's a choice you make. There are a couple baselines for having a servant's heart. First, give the customer what they pay for. If they're paying for a dozen eggs and come to you saying there are only eleven in their carton, you need to immediately replace that missing egg because they paid for a minimum of twelve eggs.

Second to having a servant's heart is to remember that it doesn't cost anything to smile. I don't have a million-dollar smile, but smiling is the easiest way to say, "I'm happy to be here and happy that you're here, too." A smile says so much without saying a word and can transform your interaction with a customer.

Third, move with a sense of urgency. Moving swiftly with a sense of purpose is the fastest way to show a customer you have a servant's heart. I don't mean you should rush through your task and do a sloppy job, but you should work with enough urgency to say, "I respect you and your time, and I want to get you in and out of here as quickly as possible so you can get on with your day." Helping a customer continue with their day is one of the greatest gifts you can give them. There will always be chatty customers who want to talk all day, but you need to find the balance between making sure they're not hurt and making sure the ten people behind them in line don't feel like you're wasting their time.

These are the key parts of the equation to having a servant's heart: smile, give them what they paid for, and move with a sense of urgency. You want a customer to leave feeling like you served them efficiently, accurately, and kindly. You might feel justified being rude to a customer, but doing so will come back to bite you. I've worked with many people who hated customers and treated them like annoying, colossal inconveniences. Unsurprisingly, their customers complained to their bosses.

When you're nice to customers, most of them will take it in stride, but occasionally, they'll come back to thank you. One time, I was waiting to open a bank account and didn't get served for over an hour. Luckily, I knew how long banking procedures could take, and I had planned accordingly. Finally, I reached the front of the line and gave my details and card to the bank teller.

As we were finishing up, the little old Hispanic lady behind the counter leaned over and said to me, "I just want to commend you for being so patient and nice." I told her I knew what it was like to serve customers, and that I'd made a vow to never be a jerk customer because I knew the other person was working hard and trying their best to help me.

The old lady reminded me a little of my mother, and I thought to myself how terrible it was that she was thankful I didn't get angry and yell at the workers. Someone not yelling made her day. I've noticed anyone who has served as a waiter or bartender usually shows a higher level of respect when they're on the other side of the table, because when you know what it's like to have people yell at you, it changes you. Having a servant's heart is a way to pay forward the respect people show you, so don't miss an opportunity.

TYPES OF INTERNAL CUSTOMERS

People don't think about internal customers, but we often work with them every day. For example, if you're a manager, your team is the customer. When you join a team, you need to think about who your customer is, and also, whose customer are you? When you look at the world from a customer service perspective, it can help you plan your career.

At a company called Bane Consulting, they don't promote people simply for being high-performing achievers; they use Net Promoter scores. Their theory is that it's not good enough to perform your job well; you need to be a good customer and be good at handling customers. Bane assesses this by conducting a survey with all their employees that amounts to peer review. For example, if someone in billing hits all their quotas and gets along well with their teammates, but the survey shows that all customers who deal with them hate them, they won't get a promotion.

At Rackspace, we ended up using Net Promoter scores for a season to evaluate each other as customers. Suddenly, I had a chance to tell the sales guy who only brought me terrible deals, lied all the time, and overpromised everything what an awful customer he was to me. It wasn't enough for the sales guy to sell ten thousand dollars in revenue—he had to be a good internal customer, too. Adopting the Net Promoter score changed the way I look at working with other departments. You need to treat them with a servant's heart as much as you would treat any external customer.

Looking back, my most vivid story about having a servant's heart took place when I moved from Gateway to Rackspace. I made the move because one of my mentors and great friends, James Brehm, worked at Rackspace. One day, he called me out of the blue and told me I should come to Rackspace, and I did. Over ten years later, he told me the story of why he referred me.

James and I were talking about serving customers when I vented how "these young kids these days don't understand about serving customers." He looked at me and asked me if I knew why he referred me to Rackspace. I told him I didn't know. James said, "Back when we were working at the Gateway store and you were a receptionist, we had a section called the Kids' Center." I remembered; Gateway was laid out as a large showroom and it was my job to put customers on a list when they came in.

I'd greet customers and give them a little spiel, offer them water or coffee, and tell them how long they could expect to wait. I'd put people on the list, make phone calls, clean the displays, and do other grunt work, but I loved my job because I got to learn about computers. The store had a kids' center where children could play with toys while their parents shopped for computers.

I didn't remember the story James told me, but apparently, we were working one day, and James was one of four or five sales reps. We were all standing around talking when somebody came around the corner and said a kid had just vomited in the kids' section. As James tells it, before anybody else could do anything, I immediately went to clean up the mess. I don't remember that story, but it left such an impression on James that he later referred me to Rackspace. Like I mentioned earlier, one of Rackspace's core values is fanatical support, and that value made James think back to the nineteen-year-old kid who didn't think twice about cleaning up vomit in the kids' center. He could see I was there to serve and I wasn't going to try and get out of the work.

I was so thankful that James told me the story and that he noticed my work ethic. It proves that when you have a servant's heart, people remember you serving. That kid who threw up doesn't know it, but he helped change my career and my life by giving me the chance to show my servant's heart. As a young professional, the question for you is this: Where can you serve? What is the kid's-vomit equivalent in your work? Find your servant's heart and own it. Someone is going to notice, but even if they don't, having a servant's heart is still a good outlook on life.

TACTICS FOR DEALING WITH CUSTOMERS

When I was promoted to the project manager position at

Rackspace, I learned under a man named John Lionato. John was a Six Sigma Black Belt teacher and told me about something called the Kano Model, which is a methodology for customer service. The model introduces many concepts, but the two I remember the most are the ideas of "must-haves" and "delighters."

If you work at Starbucks, the must-haves are you need to have coffee and cups. Those are the bare minimum things you need for customer service. Offering free Wi-Fi is considered a delighter—it's something a company doesn't need to offer, but chooses to because it delights their customers. Starbucks offers free Wi-Fi, not because their customers need it, but because the customer experience is improved when customers can Facebook stalk their friends and look at kitten photos while they enjoy their delicious cup of coffee.

In every job, there are must-haves and there are delighter moments. When you start a new job, the first thing you need to do is identify the must-haves. Often, the must-haves are things like policies and legal restrictions you need to follow. There should also be a whole category of delighters. Delighters are what set the A-players apart from the B- and C-players. The A-players go out of their way to hunt down the delighters and bring them to their customers, whether internal or external.

When I worked at H-E-B as a bagger, one of the must-haves

was that you didn't put the frozen foods with the detergents, and you didn't put the soap with the meat. You also didn't bang the bread, tomatoes, or bananas, or you'd end up with bruised and squashed products. They were the must-have rules and the baseline for being a good bagger. Then, there were the delighters.

I worked the checkout stand at H-E-B Number Five, and the thing about being a checker in Texas is that you need to go through special training. During checker training, it's the instructor's job to put the fear of God into you regarding a department called the TABC (Texas Alcoholic Beverage Commission). Their objective is to get you to card everybody in your store who buys alcohol or tobacco, and they told us a horror story about how, one day, we weren't going to card someone because we thought they were over twenty-one. They said, when that happens, the TABC is going to find the only sixteen-year-old in your city who looks forty-eight and wears a fully grown beard. They're going to send that kid to your checkout stand with a six-pack of Bud Light and you're not going to card him because he looks forty-eight, and then they're going to come in and arrest you.

Naturally, when I worked the checkout stand, I lived in fear that the bearded TABC man was going to come into my store to test me and wreck my life. I began to think every old man was the freak of nature who looked sixty-four but was really a freshman at Jefferson High School. Carding anyone who looked under twenty-one was a must-have in the Kano Model, but I did exactly what the trainers hoped I would do: I carded everyone. One day, I was working the quick check line and had a moment of panic when I saw a woman a few people down my line. She was buying a six-pack of Heineken beer, and I couldn't tell if she was over twenty-one.

Now, my Tia Elsa was always the person who gave me sage wisdom when it came to women. My sisters and I used to spend the night at her house when we visited Laredo, which was every other weekend. The best part of Tia Elsa's advice was that it always came at random times and was in no way related to whatever we were doing at the time. We'd be eating pork chops with mashed potatoes when Tia Elsa would round the corner out of the bathroom with her face covered in some kind of green cream.

She'd loudly declare as she passed, "Lencho, listen to me. When it comes to women, just remember that beauty is pain."

"Yes, ma'am."

"And remember, you *never* ask a woman her age. Never, Mijo."

"Yes, ma'am."

I didn't understand the nuance of her advice, but I could break down conceptually that asking a woman's age was offensive in some way. I cached the tip in the back of the old database and moved on with my day. Then, this one day when I couldn't tell if the woman in my line was twenty-one, all my Tia Elsa training came rushing back to me in a lesson that no one ever tells you about or can prep you to face.

If this woman had been carrying wine, it would have been a dead giveaway, because I had only ever seen older women drink wine. Heineken was a tricky one because it's a specialty beer: a slightly sophisticated beer for a young person or just a normal beer for an older person. Keep in mind when I say older, I mean people of drinking age, because at the time, I was only a teenager.

I panicked and didn't know what to do. Was she a normal woman of drinking age who wanted a nice, cold Heineken, or was she the elusive TABC unicorn who looked just old enough to get me arrested for selling to a minor? I was so young and had so much left to do—I couldn't risk it and get fired for her! Sure, I was only making $8.50 an hour, but that was big money back then.

She had unloaded her basket, and the moment of truth was approaching. What was I going to do? If I carded her and she was over twenty-one, I was sure she'd be pissed. It didn't matter. I told myself, "Don't get busted by the TABC. Just card her, and you'll feel better about the whole thing. Okay, here comes the trust fall."

I remember it like it was yesterday. The woman was so flustered and distracted. I could tell her mind was in ten different places, and there I was, about to interrupt it all to ask her age—breaking one of the cardinal rules of Tia Elsa. I started to scan her items, waiting to ring up the beer last. Meanwhile, she fumbled through her purse, checked her watch, and stared off into space like she had the weight of the world on her shoulders. Then, I scanned the beer.

I paused, tightened my stomach, grinded my teeth, and then interrupted her train of thought.

"Ma'am? Ma'am? Excuse me, ma'am?"

"Oh, sorry, I was somewhere else."

"I'm so sorry to do this but..."

"Yes?"

"I need to see your ID. For the beer, I mean."

I stopped her right in her tracks—stunned her, but hadn't dropped her to the mat. She leaned back and stared me straight in the eye. Petrified, I just stared back. Likely only three seconds passed, but it felt like five minutes. I was sure the slap was coming. *What have I done?* I thought, as Tia Elsa's voice scolded me in my head in a rapid fire of machine-gun Spanish that thankfully, I couldn't understand.

Then, the woman came back to life.

Her shocked look transformed into the biggest smile I have ever seen. "Really?" she asked as her grin continued to grow. I grew more confused by the moment as I watched a metamorphosis happen before my eyes. Her body language changed and she swayed toward me with a flirty flick of the hair. Her body, which had been tense and hurried, all of a sudden became like Jello; she looked like a marionette on a string. I was getting worried, but she grabbed her purse with glee and said, "Yes, of course you can see my ID!"

She paid and then practically skipped out of the store as I stood there completely bewildered. I looked around, and on the quick check behind me was Hilda, who had seen the whole thing go down. She could read the look of puzzlement on my face.

Hilda shook her head and told me, "You made her feel young, dummy."

I spent the rest of my shift mentally dissecting what had just happened. *Girl walks in, you card her, and she becomes happy.* Could this equation work every time, if implemented the right way? Was this a one-time occurrence, or was I on to real insight for the first time? Maybe this equation was a weapon that would give me a secret advantage.

I decided I'd use the scientific method to test this hypothesis. All I needed was another woman to come through my line and buy alcohol. Luckily for me, I lived in the hood, and there was no short supply. The second woman I carded was a layup from the start. She was obviously about forty-five years old, but I decided, *What the hell? I'll give it a shot.* When I asked for her ID, her reaction was even more explosive than the first lady's.

"Oh, sweetie, I could kiss you for asking me that. Of course, you can see my ID, darling!"

Holy crap, this is awesome, I thought. For the first time in my life, I felt like I had a superpower. For the rest of my tenure as cashier, I became the most irresponsible employee you ever saw. I didn't care about anything but carding women to refine my technique. All other humans buying alcohol were an inconvenience to me and were merely obstacles between me and the next woman I could card.

I probably would have sold alcohol to a nine-year-old if they had come through my line without carding them, but if an old lady came through with a travel-size wine bottle for making risotto, I was all over the situation. I learned quickly that there was a direct correlation between the age of the woman and the reaction I received. I also learned that if I wanted to get the most out of the event, I had to become somewhat of a showman. The more I slowed down the interaction and showed concern, the more dramatic it would be. For example:

"Ma'am, I'm sorry." Long, concerned pause. "I'm afraid I'm gonna need to see your ID."

From then on, the equation was simple:

Woman + Alcohol + Dramatic pause + Concerned look × Identification check = Happy lady

To be clear, I never picked anyone up or got anyone's phone number. At that time in my life, I wouldn't have known what to do if someone actually tried to flirt back with me. I probably would have peed my pants. The quick check line is where I learned how to flirt, and what made the whole thing so fun was that the story was always the same. Each woman would come through my line with no idea what was about to hit them. They all seemed to be one million miles away, and no matter where they were, my question was about to change the trajectory of their day for the better.

Man, it was a good feeling. The lesson here is that, at first, I was looking at the world from the business's point of view, but when you look at the world from the customers' perspective, it changes everything. Always view the world from their perspective. This is the Kano Model difference between must-haves and delighter moments. I didn't have to card women who were clearly over the age of twenty-one, but I did it because I knew it would make them happy.

My question to you is this: How can you delight your customers? Customers get a sense for people who enjoy their work, and seeing someone who wants to serve them inspires loyalty. You may not realize it, but there exists a way for you to change the trajectory of their day. Go and find the delighters, because they make work—and the world—so much better.

IS THIS THE HILL YOU WANT TO DIE ON?

When figuring out how to handle a potential confrontation, especially when it involves a customer, I like to ask a question from my best friend, Dax Moreno: **Is this the hill you want to die on?** It's about picking your battles, which is important whether you're dealing with customers, employees, teammates, or people in your personal life.

I've had to ask myself this question many times, but the most dramatic example was one particular day at H-E-B Number Five. I was working as the traffic controller, but there were almost no customers in the store, so I had time to hang out in the back. As I walked around the store, I saw a really rough-looking guy in a stained, ribbed tank top with horrible tattoo sleeves on his arms. You can tell whether someone has good ink or prison ink—this guy clearly had the latter.

He walked into the store on a mission, flying through an empty check stand and heading toward the left side of the store where we kept the bandages, medicine, and diapers. I didn't think anything of it when he walked into the baby food aisle, but a couple minutes later, he reemerged carrying about five cases, or over three hundred dollars' worth of Enfamil baby formula. I watched this guy, who could easily stomp a young Lorenzo Gomez into the ground, as he started to walk through an empty check stand. Clearly, he had no intention to pay for the formula.

I felt like time passed in slow motion as I watched this guy stroll toward the door. The loss prevention manager ran across the store, pointed at the thief, and said, "Lorenzo, stop that guy!" I looked at him, looked back at her, and then said, "You only pay me eight dollars an hour. There's no way I'm confronting that guy."

The loss prevention manager ran in front of the guy and tried to corner him, but it was funny because, legally, she wasn't allowed to touch him. He shoved the Enfamil into her hands and took off running. The principle I want to highlight is that in the moment she yelled at me to stop the guy, I was actually telling her, "Lady, this isn't the hill

I'm going to die on. Not the hill of the guy who's done hard time and is stealing food to feed his baby."

When it comes to customers, there are some things you need to go to battle over, but there are many others that you can't. If a customer is arguing over a two-dollar coupon that you have the authority to approve or not, is that the hill you want to die on? If you can help a customer without breaking company policy, it's often better to give them that battle, especially when it's over something as small as two dollars.

Later in my career, there were many times when I suddenly had the authority to do something like give customers free shipping. If a customer had just received terrible service from another employee, I'd usually use that authority to make their experience a little better, because small things like free shipping can go a long way.

If you're going to go to battle with someone in your department, like a manager you hate, or if there's an issue you want to fight for, you need to ask yourself, "Is this the hill I want to die on?" Is this issue worth the trouble I might bring upon myself? Think about your answer carefully, because I'm here to tell you that most of the time, whatever it is won't be the hill you want to die on.

I can only think of one instance in my career when I looked at the situation and said, "This is the hill I'm prepared to die on." It was an issue that went against my core beliefs. I thought something unethical was happening, and I was going to fight to make it right, even if I got fired in the end. It was an important issue, but I want to save you the hassle of making confrontational decisions involving small, everyday issues.

You're going to have customers, your boss, and your teammates asking you to do things you don't want to do. You can get into a fight every time, or you can ask yourself, "Is that the hill I want to die on?" My advice is to save the battles for when it counts.

IF YOU'RE GOING TO KILL THE KING, YOU BETTER KILL THE KING

There will be times in your career when you have a boss you absolutely hate. You may even have to pick a battle with that person, but here's the advice I heard from Graham, **"If you're going to kill the king, you better kill the king.** In other words, if you take on your boss or another higher-up at your company and don't get rid of him, he'll come after you. To use *Game of Thrones* as an example, they tried to kill Khaleesi and failed; now she's coming back with three dragons.

This is the one story that makes me most ashamed, and if I could go back in time and do something differently in my entire career, it's this series of events. I'm going to tell you because it is my hope that I can help you avoid making the same mistake.

A few years into my tech career, I didn't get along with my manager. There was no reason we shouldn't have gotten along; we used to be teammates and had a blast working together. In fact, I had trained this guy when he started out at the company. Then, because he was more mature and ambitious than me, he pursued a leadership position.

I was a snot-nosed punk who thought the world should've just noticed how amazing I was and made me a manager. But that is not how the world works, and one day, they made this guy a manager—my manager. Now, I had a peer who I trained telling me what to do. There is no other way for me to say this except to say, I became a fool. I was so immature and hurt that I lashed out and became an absolute jerk to this guy, doing everything I could to let him know I didn't respect him.

This role was also one of his first leadership experiences, and as you can imagine, my bad attitude went down like a shit sandwich. He upped the pressure on me, and I upped my defiance. On and on, we played this game of chicken until, one day, I took the nuclear option. I went on a campaign to get him removed from our team.

Just like Absalom standing at the city gate, I pitched my

case to my team. I whispered in their ears at every chance I got: in the break room, during lunch time, and even at the smokers' corner. Eventually, I won everyone to my side and had the entire team fired up. I thought that, surely, they would make this guy move teams or even fire him, but that is not what happened.

In hindsight, the guy had done nothing wrong, but he now had an entire team on the path to mutiny. We also happened to be the highest performing team in the division. It was an explosive situation.

The day it came to a head, I felt confident I'd get my way, but I did not kill the king. Our vice president was smart and loyal to his new manager. He pulled the entire team into a room and said, "Guys, I have sent your manger home for the week. But I want you to know that I am not going to fire him, and I am not going to move him. He is not going anywhere, and we are not leaving this room until we figure out how to work together and with him."

That day in the conference room, the cold reality of the situation hit me. I had wounded the king, but I had not killed him. And now, I was in for it. I realized there was no going back, because as soon as this guy returned, he would never forget I tried to take him out. I realized I had to leave the team before he fired me. Not only did I leave the team, but I left the entire department. The move broke my heart, because I'd been on the winning team and wanted to win with them for years. In the end, I self-destructed and got the opposite of what I wanted.

I am here to tell you there are so few times in your career when you should try to kill the king. For most of you reading this book, the answer as to when to do it is actually never. Most of the time, you should run in the opposite direction. Only when there are real ethical or legal infractions should you take up the banner and go after the king, but most of the time, there will never be a need. If you are the one-in-a-million person who needs to kill the king, you better get the job done. Otherwise, you're the one who will get taken out.

THE 80/20 PRINCIPLE

One of my favorite principles about customers I learned from a book called *The 80/20 Principle: The Secret to Achieving More with Less* by Richard Koch. The first time I heard about the principle in a real-life setting was during a Rackspace Open Book session with the CEO. He informed us that 20 percent of our customers accounted for over 80 percent of our revenue. We decided to launch an initiative to separate the higher-value customers into another department to give them special service.

The initiative ended up being a huge revenue generator for Rackspace, and it was all based on the 80/20 Principle, or what is called Pareto's Principle in academic circles. The principle originated in the late 1800s from an Italian economist named Vilfredo Pareto. Pareto discovered that 20 percent of Italy's citizens owned 80 percent of the country's wealth. He found that this ratio applied to everything in the world and asserted that few inputs equal maximum output.

From a team perspective, 20 percent of the employees typically account for 80 percent of the work. To impress your manager, you want to make sure you're in that 20 percent. The 80/20 ratio is at play all around us, in every work environment, with teams, managers, and especially customers. No matter where you work, there will always be a few customers who take up more than their proportional share of your time. Simply put, there will be a few customers who are a pain in the ass to serve. There will also be a few customers who make everything worth it and are an absolute delight.

I've had two customers who stood out as fitting the 80/20 Principle exceptionally well. The first was a bad customer named Otto. Otto was a huge, balding Anglo guy who shopped at the Handy Andy in the Hispanic neighborhood and drove an ugly, beat-up green truck. He had long fingernails, and in my head, he was a Sith Lord, so all of these characteristics made him stand out.

On top of everything else, Otto was mean. He was the first customer I encountered who had no patience and would yell at the workers. I thought Otto was a terrible customer, but I realized I had to serve him, so I did. I would help carry his groceries to his car and, eventually, got to the point where Otto was very civil with me.

It occurred to me that there weren't a lot of Ottos—there was just one Otto and, every once in a while, another bad customer. However rare, you need to be prepared to deal with Otto; otherwise, he can ruin your day. On the other side of the spectrum, there was a large, Anglo woman who stood out like Otto. I expected her to be mean like Otto, but when I bagged her groceries, she was quiet. Quiet doesn't mean nice, necessarily, nor does it always mean snobby. Some people are simply quiet.

While prematurely judging the woman, I bagged her groceries and took them to her car. Then, she thanked me and handed me three dollars. It was the first time in my career that I'd ever been tipped by a customer. I stood in that parking lot feeling ashamed of myself and so touched by this woman whom I'd completely misjudged. She was in the 20 percent of customers who value the people helping them and treat people with respect. Otto was in the 20 percent of bad customers, but the bad and good balance each other. My interaction with the woman taught me to not judge people too quickly, because you can't tell the content of someone's character by how they look.

When it comes to customers, 20 percent will be amazing, 20 percent will be terrible, and there will be all kinds of people in between. With this principle and all the others, it's important to remember there are shades of gray. We live in a nuanced world, and my goal is to give you some tools to sift through the gray areas and come to your own conclusions. If you treat everyone equally with a servant's heart, you'll be off to a good start.

EVERYONE'S IN SALES

"Everybody has to sell themselves and their ideas."

—GRAHAM WESTON

In the same way that everyone, regardless of your position, is in customer service, everyone is also in sales. Learning this in the real world was certainly a shock for me, as I'm naturally sales averse—I think most people are the same—but nonetheless, I found myself working in sales.

The realization crystallized for me when I started working for Graham's 80/20 Foundation. We made a grant to a sales program at the Texas A&M University, which seemed odd to me because it was in the Agricultural Economics Department. I attended a meeting with Graham and several Ag-Econ professors talking about the price of corn, and I remember thinking, *I'm such a city slicker. I have no idea what these guys are talking about.* The subject wasn't my area of expertise at all, but I found it fascinating. I found out that Graham had received his bachelor of science degree from A&M's Agricultural Economics Department, and while he was a student there, a professor named Dr. Kerry Litzenberg realized everyone is in sales. The professor made it a requirement that all Ag-Econ students take a sales class, and Graham said the class had changed his career.

Many years later, Graham and I went to A&M to give them a grant that would beef up the Ag-Econ sales program. As I was sitting at the back of the classroom, which felt odd because I'm a college dropout, Graham talked to a group of college students. He said something that's never left me, which was, "Everybody's in sales. Whether you know it or not, even if you aren't selling a product, **you have to sell yourself and your ideas**." It's a great principle that holds true in business and life.

In the context of work and customers, I believe it's always best to serve first and sell second. Serving should be the basis for everything you do in business, especially with customers. Sometimes, selling is a by-product of serving in that you can serve your customers by selling them what they need to make their lives better.

The problem with sales is it has a bad brand. When you think of the word *sales*, you probably think of a pushy used-car salesperson who is focused solely on closing the deal as soon as you step on the lot—someone who's trying to pull one over on you with ridiculous, sleazy tactics. It doesn't help when movies like *Boiler Room* show Ben Affleck throwing his Ferrari keys on the table while proclaiming, "We're here to shove our product down customers' throats."

I'm here to tell you that most of the negative stereotypes about sales are untrue. In fact, the sales people I've worked with are some of the smartest, hardest-working people I've ever met. There's a science to good sales, and it's what makes companies grow. When done correctly, sales can be a thing of beauty.

I didn't see the good side of sales until I started progressing in my career. One of the things that held me back was my first job in sales, which nobody ever explained to me. When I was at Gateway, I worked as a receptionist and then got promoted to sales. I knew sales wasn't my strength, but I didn't have the fortitude to sell myself or my ideas in order to sell myself out of being in sales. I was stuck in that role, and while I was stuck, I was Gateway's worst sales guy in all of human history. I don't think I ever hit my goal once, and the only reason they kept me around is because everybody liked me, which only made the situation worse—it was just terrible to have the pity position.

The first lesson of sales that nobody taught me was about selling value. Gateway was famous for selling their computers in cow-spotted boxes as a nod back to the company's roots in a barn in Sioux City, Iowa. In the retail stores, we'd demo the products, make a sale, and then ship the computer to the customer. To me, making a sale was all about the transaction, and I didn't understand that a real sales person aims to solve a customer's problem by providing a solution. For example, "Oh, you have a headache? This Tylenol will make it go away," represents the true essence of sales.

The best example of my failings as a salesperson involved the warranty. All of Gateway's displays showed a three-year warranty, even though the default was one year. When a customer would ask me, "Can I get a cheaper price?" I'd immediately answer, "Yeah, you can reduce the warranty, which will save you two hundred dollars." I didn't think there was value in the warranty and only focused on facilitating the transaction.

My buddy Luke, on the other hand, understood value and how to be a good salesperson. If you were to ask Luke the same question about lowering the price, he'd reply, "No, you need the warranty, and let me tell you why. You need the warranty because you're going to use this computer a lot, and the more you use it, the more likely it is to break. You want the warranty so you can come back here in a few years and we'll fix it for free."

Luke had been working with computers since before the birth of the Internet, so he truly appreciated the importance of a warranty and was able to sell its value. Luke hit his quota every month, while I sat there in the corner feeling sorry for myself. I created a narrative in my mind that all salespeople bent the truth a bit—which is completely untrue—and went home with my pity party. I told my dad, "Pops, I don't think it's possible to be a good sales guy and be honest." He looked at me and replied, "Well, then be a bad sales guy, but be honest."

Later, I understood that Luke hadn't bent the truth; I simply didn't understand how to sell value. It was my problem rather than a problem with the sales profession as a whole. Sales aren't bad; sales are essential. A small percentage of salespeople have given the entire industry a bad brand, but most salespeople are great. If you work in sales, ask yourself how you can sell value to your customers and how you can solve their problems.

Fortunately, when I moved to Rackspace and took the role of account manager, I completely blossomed. One of my responsibilities was selling, but there was a difference. As an account manager at Rackspace, I didn't have a quota to hit. I could sell without the pressure, which allowed me to relax. I could tell a customer, "Ma'am, your hard drive's full. You need to buy more space, so I'm going to make the upgrade for you." The company would make a sale, and I'd solve a customer's problem.

Rackspace realized there were people who thrived under the pressure of competing to hit a quota every month, and then there were people like me who shrank under the pressure of a quota and cared more about building a relationship with a customer. Rackspace knew they needed a position to suit each strength, so they got rid of the position of "account manager" and created a new one called the "business development consultant," whose job it was to sell to current customers.

They paired me with a sales legend at Rackspace named Vladimir Mata, aka Locon. Vlad and I were the first beta experiment of this pairing, where one of us handled the customer relationship and the other person, which in our case was Vlad, negotiated contracts and upsold the customer to hit a quota. Our partnership worked extremely well. Vlad and I were like Batman and Robin, a dynamic duo. As unstoppable as Godzilla. We crushed the experiment so well, Rackspace rolled the model out to the entire company. When I went to London, part of my role was to implement this new innovation in the UK office.

Vlad and I worked well together because we had a social agreement. When there were small, easy sale items that I knew customers needed, I'd take care of them for Vlad, and it would go towards his quota. Vlad came in to handle all the high-pressure sales, because he loved the intensity. Working with Vlad made me recognize a few principles that I want to break down. First, true salespeople love to compete.

Most people think those who work in sales are only moti-vated by money, but that's not true. Some salespeople are motivated by money, but a huge portion of them get up every day to win. You could make a twelve-ounce bottle of soda the prize, and salespeople would kill each other to win it, because their motivation comes from competing.

THE HIGH-RISK, HIGH-REWARD WORLD OF SALES

Salespeople operate under an obscene amount of pressure to hit their quotas and have the most black-and-white role in the entire organization. They either hit their quota, or they don't, and if they miss it for several months, they get fired. Nowhere else in any company is someone's role that simple. Due to the stress they experience, salespeople get paid what my old boss in the UK, Andrew Gibbens, used to call "the danger money."

Salespeople are, and should be, some of the highest-paid people in an organization because they go through the stress no one else wants to face. Every company needs an army of salespeople pushing their products, because when you look at the numbers, half the reason the rest of us get our paychecks is because the salespeople are carrying the weight. Salespeople are extremely important.

When I first became the CEO of Geekdom, a San Antonio-based coworking space, I realized I needed to hire a sales rep. I brought my team together and explained that I didn't know who the sales rep would be yet, but when they joined the team, they'd be the highest-paid person there. They'd probably make more than me when they hit their quota, and it's because no one else wanted the stress I was about to put on that person.

As a young professional, I want you to know you shouldn't resent the salespeople for their salaries when you run into them. They perform a job that's high stress and highly competitive. If you happen to be highly competitive and thrive under pressure, you should probably consider a job in sales. But believe me when I say, the sales lifestyle is not for everybody.

NEVER SELL AN IDEA WITH "I THINK"

I moved to London and lived there from 2004–2006 while working at Rackspace. During my time there, I lived with a guy named Matt Schatz, who is one of the greatest sales leaders I've met in my entire life. Matt taught me a lot about sales, in particular, about selling yourself. London was the second most expensive city to live in at the time, and Matt knew how relatively poorly they paid me. When Rackspace went through a hiring period to bring on a lot of new salespeople, he began to sell me on the idea of coming over to the sales team.

The sales position paid more, but I knew in my gut I wasn't

a good salesperson. Unfortunately, I couldn't articulate my argument, and because I couldn't sell myself, Matt sold me instead. He convinced me to move to sales, so I transferred from account management, where I was amazing, and became Rackspace's worst sales guy of all time, just like I had been at Gateway.

Matt Schatz is one of my closest friends and had no bad intentions. As a matter of fact, he tried to help me make more money. The problem was that he was better at selling himself and his ideas than I was at selling mine. Luckily, not long after floundering in sales, he transferred me back to serving customers. In hindsight, I should've done a better job of selling myself.

I should've told Matt that the money really didn't matter to me, that I was okay being poor, and that I didn't perform my best when I had the pressure of a quota. My strengths are serving customers by helping them, rather than trying to sell them value. Solving customers' problems made me happy, and the best way to build long-lasting relationships with them was to be an account manager. In essence, I should've sold myself, but I did not.

To avoid making my mistake, it's important for you to understand who you are and what your strengths are. When you identify those factors, you can sell yourself to people, which will bring about the best outcome for both you and the company hiring you. My second piece of advice is to sell yourself with actions and use words when necessary. In simpler terms, show, don't tell. Don't tell people you're a hard worker; show them you're a hard worker. Don't tell people you're smart; show them you're smart by solving a difficult problem. Personally, I love seeing a smart, new employee come up with a good idea, implement it, and fix something that's been broken for years. It's an action that shows the person's intelligence and value to the company.

For managers or people who want to be managers, don't tell people you're a leader—just lead. Nobody needs to deputize you to be a leader, and if you lead, people will notice. There are leaders all over the place who were never deputized and don't have the title, but they lead their teams nonetheless. When you work so hard that you become a misallocation of resources, your company will need to promote you.

If you sell yourself with actions first, the words and recognition will come. People need to recognize this principle, especially when they want to sell themselves on a resume. On a resume, you'll get the best results by giving specific examples of your successful actions. For example, don't say you're a great salesperson; describe how you increased revenue for your company 10 percent last year.

Now you know how to sell yourself, but how do you sell your ideas? Selling your ideas is a skill I've had to learn by managing people, and the most important principle I want to tell you about is this: "I think" is the worst way to sell an idea. When you say, "I think," or, "I don't know, but I think this is right," you're doing the worst job on planet Earth of selling your idea. The words, "I think," undermine any authority you might have conveyed.

The cool thing about selling an idea is it's one of the few times in life when it's okay to copy someone else, because the best ideas come from referencing experts, mashing two ideas together, and making their ideas into a new idea. It's the one time in life when you can ignore your high school English teachers and copy off your neighbor. The caveat is you need to admit when you're copying.

When I started working at Geekdom, I realized designing a nice space for people to sit and work was important, but it also needed to be functional. You couldn't have the space grow too loud, provide desks that were too small, or offer Wi-Fi that was too weak. Everything needed to work in a certain way. Geekdom grew rapidly, and before long, we had two floors of an eight-story building and were about to take over a third floor.

Two of my teammates helped me design the space and choose the furniture, but they were design snobs who cared more about the aesthetic value than the function. They gave me a proposal for the layout, but I told them, "This is wrong, and here's why." I laid out my argument with a bunch of data points to support my claim. Then I asked them, "Why would you choose the layout you're suggesting?"

Nobody could give me an answer. I gave them my proposal, and all they responded with was, "I don't think that's right. I don't like it." But they couldn't articulate why or defend their ideas. When you tell someone, "I just don't think it's right," you lose credibility. My coworkers didn't like my design, but they couldn't back up their opinion with any data. Without data, their opinions were as useful to me as a Magic 8-Ball.

When you don't have data to back up your ideas, you're always going to get outranked by an idea that does. In the design scenario, I told my teammate we weren't using her idea because she couldn't defend it. I came into the discussion having read three books on workspace design and having studied other numerous coworking spaces, but all my coworkers brought to the table were their preferences. You don't need a full scientific study to support your point, but show the person you're trying to convince that you've read a book, listened to a podcast, or watched a TED Talk; anything that shows you have given this project some thought outside of your eight-to-five job.

"I don't think it's right," isn't a strong argument, and you never want to be the person saying it in the workplace. Supporting an argument relates back to the previous rule of "show, don't tell." Show any type of data at your disposal, even if it's something like a Pinterest board of other people's ideas. Showing something at least proves you've been thinking about the problem, so go out and find books, studies, precedents, and more. You want to show that the world has an answer to your problem and you've attempted to find it. Anything is better than, "I think."

In the same scenario, I let my teammates order approximately eighty desks for our production floor. The night the desks were delivered, which was the weekend before we planned to open the floor, I immediately realized something was wrong—the desks were too big. I asked why we ordered the big desks instead of the regular size. My coworker replied, "Well, we thought we'd get the bigger desks. They can seat more people." I asked him to pull two chairs up to the desk and we both sat. The space was so cramped, our elbows almost touched. I said, "We work in a coworking space. Are you going to sit this close to a stranger? This is way too intimate." My coworker realized he'd made a mistake by going with "I think," whereas I went with experience and data. The reason I knew our old desks were the right size was because I had three years of data showing me that lots of people sat at them.

Everybody sells themselves and their ideas, and you need to figure out how to do so effectively. What are your strengths? What do you enjoy? What are you bad at doing? All kinds of tools exist to help you answer these questions, such as the Myers-Briggs test or Strengths Finder assessment. Once you identify your strengths, start preparing to sell your ideas. PowerPoint is one of the lamest corporate tools in existence, but it's extremely powerful. When you're making an argument, put all your ideas in PowerPoint, add bullet points, explain your reasoning, and provide supporting documents. I've outgunned people who are much smarter than me simply by taking the time to research the problem, show my supporting data, and propose at least one solution. Sell your ideas correctly, and there's no stopping how far you can go in your career.

THE POWER OF STORY

If selling an idea is an equation, there is one last variable you need for the formula to work. I have told you to do research and to have data that supports your strategy. All of that is great, but one variable is a force multiplier and that variable is story.

Around 2012, I was invited to join Graham at the annual XPRIZE Foundation Visioneering Conference, an event where innovative people get together to try to solve some of the world's grand challenges. As you can imagine, they really wanted Graham to attend, not me. However, when Graham told them I was the guy who handled the money at the foundation, they were excited to have me tag along.

The conference was only a couple of days, but it felt like it lasted two weeks. It was one of the times in my career where I was clearly in the presence of superlativeness. Arianna Huffington was there. Paul Allen, the cofounder of Microsoft, was there. Even the actor who played Dwight from the US version of *The Office* was there, Rainn Wilson.

For one of the workshops at the conference, we had to break up into small groups of five or six and pitch a big idea that would help humanity. Naturally, Graham and I were on a team, but mostly because I was too intimidated to leave his side. At the end of the workshop, each team had to pick a spokesperson to pitch their world-changing, made-up idea to the bigger group. We chose Graham.

What happened next left such an impression on me that it changed how I sell ideas today. I was standing behind Graham, and right before he got up to pitch, he leaned his head back over his shoulder and whispered to me, "I've found that people only remember stories, so I am going to tell them a story."

He walked onto the stage and addressed the crowd. "Last summer, my sons and I took a road trip from San Antonio to Florida, and the entire way there, one of my sons played Angry Birds. He played the game the entire way. Here is my idea: What if we could make learning as addictive as Angry Birds? My idea is called Addictive Learning." For that round of pitches, Graham absolutely smoked everyone else.

The makers of Angry Birds have no idea how much they helped me sell ideas after that day.

If you want to sell an idea, do the research and have your data points ready. But if you want to ram your idea into the end zone, then tell a story that puts you over the top.

NEVER USE THE SQUEEZE PLAY

The more you advance in your career, the more complicated negotiating becomes. Just like sales, negotiating has been misbranded. I used to think negotiating meant acting like Ari Gold from *Entourage*—you'd go into the meeting with a ton of aggression and tell people, "This is what's going to happen." The real world doesn't work that way. Negotiating is not about being Ari Gold from *Entourage*; it's about understanding what's happening and how to reach a compromise or solution.

A piece of excellent advice from one of my board members, Khaled, is to **never use the Squeeze Play** when negotiating. What is the Squeeze Play? It's using ultimatums and threats to get your way. Someone using the Squeeze Play might say, "You're going to give me a deal or else. You're going to do X, Y, and Z, or I'm going to do A, B, and C." The Squeeze Play says, "You don't have a choice. I'm forcing my will on you." Once you pull that move, you've already lost the negotiation. The Squeeze Play never succeeds at anything but making people mad at you. The result of a negotiation should not be to create a loser, but a partner. The Squeeze Play forces someone to overtly be the loser, and that is no good for anyone.

At one point in my career, I consulted with Khaled. I was all worked up because I knew a nonprofit was going to ask my boss Graham for a grant, but they weren't a charity that was in our scope. They planned to circumvent me and go straight to Graham, which made me furious. I vented to Khaled and said, "I'm going to tell Graham if he gives that nonprofit the money, I'm just going to quit. Because if he does that, why am I even here?" Khaled looked me square in the eye as a board member and said, "Eso, never use the Squeeze Play. It won't get you what you want from Graham."

I realized I was being a moron and adjusted my tactic before talking with Graham. We met and I said, "Graham, I'm going to be honest. There's this nonprofit that's going to ask you for money, and I'm already stressed about it. I'm worried they're going to jump through some serious mental-gymnastic hoops to convince you. Can we agree, because they're not in our scope, that we won't give them the money?"

Graham said, "Of course."

Just like that, this fantasy I'd built in my head was completely shattered. I was so worked up that I thought the only recourse I had was to go in and use the Squeeze Play on Graham, but I'm so glad I didn't. The Squeeze Play never works. It will ruin your career and drive away your board members, so leave it in the toolbox.

Veto power applies to vetoing bad ideas, but it also plays a role in negotiations. I learned about veto power from Graham, who learned about it from his negotiating coach, Coach Jim Camp. Camp wrote a famous book about negotiations titled *Start with No*. According to Coach, if the other person feels like they don't have veto power, you've lost the negotiation. This concept goes against everything the world has taught us about negotiations, which is to dig your heels in and steamroll the other person into submission.

A much better approach to negotiations is for everybody involved to have veto power and the option to walk away from the deal. You never want to make the situation binary rather than give the other person options; otherwise, they'll feel cornered. Everyone needs to know they have some degree of control over the outcome, including you. When the balance shifts too much in one person's favor, the negotiation has already failed.

DON'T SPEND WHAT YOU EARN

―――

"The bill comes due."

— DR. STRANGE

I read an amazing book by a pastor named Andy Stanley, titled *The Principle of the Path*. I feel like no one has ever articulated this financial principle better, which is, "Nobody wakes up in ruin by accident." Stanley also wrote, "Direction, not intention, leads to your destination." The idea is that everything you do takes you a step in some direction, so which direction are you headed in?

For example, you might decide to buy a new car when you

get a raise—which is something I did when I was younger. I was working at Rackspace and had just gotten a promotion when the Nissan 350Z came out. One day, one of my coworkers, an engineer named Tim, showed me the car. With me being young, dumb, and clueless about the world, I became entirely swept up in the awesomeness of it. I fell into the trap of thinking, "If I had that car, everything would be better."

As soon as I got the raise, Dax and I ran out to the dealer, and I leased a brand new 350Z. It was a gorgeous car—shiny black paint with burnt-orange leather seats. Now, I was not prepared for a $500 monthly car payment, but I got the car anyway. I didn't care. I should note that this car was wasted on me; I'm the slowest grandma ever behind the wheel. Guys would pull up next to me and rev their engines, wanting to race. I'd shoot them a look that said, "It's on." The light would change and they'd take off screeching, while I just slowly rolled around a turn.

One morning after getting this car, I arrived at Rackspace, and as I pulled into the garage, our CEO, Lanham, saw me. He shot me a look that said, "Are you kidding?" The car went directly against Rackspace's core value of substance over flash, and when I saw his look, I panicked. I parked and ran into the building, then barged into Lanham's office and blurted, "It's not what it looks like! I live with my brother. He doesn't charge me rent." I rattled off a few more excuses, but Lanham wasn't having any of it.

He said, "Let me tell you about depreciating assets. As soon as you drive off the lot, a car loses value. So every day you have that car, it'll be worth less." He gave me a whole lecture and really let me have it in a stern, fatherly way. I left his office thinking he hated my guts, but his talk left an impression on me, because no one had ever told me about depreciating assets before. Lanham has an MBA from Harvard, so I thought to myself, *This guy knows what he's talking about. It's really worth considering what he says.*

In the end, I sold the car to move to the UK, and while I took a loss on it, it was a learning experience. I had taken a step toward dramatically reducing my disposable income. I didn't need a 350Z with leather seats; I just needed a car that worked. When you face a similar situation, consider: you can choose to buy a used car that works or a new car that works. There's nothing wrong with buying a new car, but you've now taken a step toward stretching your paycheck a little bit further. Renting a brand-new apartment would take you another step in that direction. Then you buy a flat-screen TV, a surround-sound audio system, and a fancy sofa. You've suddenly taken many more steps toward thinning your paycheck. No matter what you do, you're headed in some direction.

People say, "I don't know how I woke up in bankruptcy or in debt." Andy Stanley's response would be, "Let's retrace your steps. You didn't have the sofa, the sound system, the TV, the apartment, and the car. What was your financial situation before all of that?" On the other hand, putting a dollar in your savings account or making an extra payment on your car loan are steps toward financial security. Every decision is a step, and you should figure out whether you're headed in the right direction.

UNDERSTANDING THE WAY THE WORLD WORKS

I've been blessed with a lot of good advice about money, especially when I first started working. When I received my first paycheck at Handy Andy, I made $4.85 an hour. I remember that number because it had a profound effect on me. I was proud to be working, but it was also humbling to see on paper what my time was worth.

I'd never been paid for work before, and it felt strange to see a value associated with my time and effort. I couldn't wait to be worth more—not that I wanted to be richer, but to know that I could personally have a hand in making that number go higher if I worked hard. Getting better at my job seemed amazing. Handy Andy used to give out their paychecks in paper check form, and I'll never forget the first time I cashed my paycheck. I stood in line at the business center with a bunch of day laborers—grown men who were construction workers, carpenters, and mechanics.

I was only a teenager with a paycheck just north of one-hundred dollars, but I stood two feet taller that day because I felt like a man. The other men in line were probably going to go do noble things and bring food home to their families, but I was just happy that I'd worked hard and earned a paycheck.

Before I got that first paycheck, my brother Danny, the chairman of my board, sat me down for a talk. He said, "Hey, Bro, I have to tell you something about your first paycheck. You need to understand that Uncle Sam is going to take a big bite out of it. There's this thing called gross and net, the money you earned and then the money that's left after everything else is paid. I'm telling you this so you won't be upset when you see that number." It was such a little insight, but I'm so glad he prepared me to face the reality that you don't get all of what you earn. It's an important truth that isn't always explained to new workers.

I asked Danny to explain social security tax. At the time, I thought social security tax meant the government took money from my paycheck and literally put it in an account for my future.

Danny said, "No, no, no, you don't understand, Bro. That money is going to other people."

I was shocked. I said, "What? My paycheck is going to other people? What about me?"

Danny replied, "Other people will pay for you in the future."

As a seventeen-year-old kid, social security was a mind-blowing concept. For the first time, I understood the social context of my paycheck in the broader scheme of the city, the state, and the nation.

Danny explained how taxes worked, but he also set my expectations. If he hadn't, I probably would've felt robbed when I first got my paycheck. In fact, I still felt a little robbed, but at least I was prepared for it and understood why it was happening. The principle of this story is you're going to work hard, but you're not going to get to keep all your money—it's not how the system works.

My brother hammered another principle into my head, which was, "Don't spend what you earn." Basically, don't overcommit yourself. Even more radical, don't spend everything you make. Always spend less than your paycheck and save some. Later in my career when I had better jobs, Danny's advice came into play more often. I'd say to myself, "I'm about to buy a new car," and hear Danny's voice asking, "Can you afford a new car? Can you afford a new car *and* a cell phone? Your wallet's getting a little thinner. Don't spend what you earn."

Perhaps more than anything else, this principle applies to credit cards. Credit cards aren't free money, and Danny made sure I understood that. He said, "Look, one day you're going to get a credit card, and when you do, you need to treat it like you don't have it. It's for emergencies only. When you treat your credit card like free money, you go into debt." He also told me, "You need to start building credit. Credit is how you get a mortgage for a house and buy a car. Once you're earning credit, always, always, always pay your bill on time."

During this lesson, Danny got really serious when he brought up his last point. All his other advice I took to heart, of course, but when he looked me straight in the eye and said, "Always pay your bills on time," I knew he meant business. The principle stuck with me, and I'm fortunate that my brother and parents did a good job of setting my expectations. They didn't want me to live paycheck to paycheck like so many people do, so they showed me a different way to look at money.

When you live paycheck to paycheck, you feel desperate, and it happens to people at all levels of income. When I watched football or basketball with my brother, he'd lean over and tell me, "You see those players? They live paycheck to paycheck. They're making a ton of money, but they're spending all of it on fancy houses and cars that they can't actually afford." Saving a little money and not living paycheck to paycheck improves your life in so many ways. Above all, you sleep better at night feeling like a responsible adult.

HOW TITHING TAUGHT ME ABOUT MONEY

One time in my life, I was asked to help in the most unexpected way. I was working at Handy Andy as a bagger and had been saving up all summer to buy a 1967 Mustang. I didn't realize the car would cost me a million dollars in upkeep and that it wouldn't make me cool, but I wanted it. By the end of the summer, I had saved $1,300, which was the most money I'd ever had to my name.

My mother came up to me one evening looking so sheepish and sad. She said, "Lencho, I was wondering if we could borrow that money you've been saving, because we need to pay our property taxes."

Several funny things happened when my mother said that. The first was that I stood there in complete shock, because my mother wasn't telling me what to do. She had come to me as though I were a man, and as a sixteen-year-old kid, I'd never experienced that treatment from my parents before. I didn't know how to handle it.

The second thing that happened is I learned there was a thing called property taxes. When my mother asked for my help, she pulled the curtain back and showed me some of the things adults have to deal with that they had been shielding me from, one of which was property taxes. The third thing that hit me was I was happy to help my mom. I didn't hesitate. I said, "Of course, you can have the money.

Of course." At that point, I was prepared to give it to her and never see it again, but she ended up paying me back with no problem. To this day, it remains such a heavy moment in my life, because I was so proud to give back to the universe.

The experience made my mom a human being. My mom had always been my mom—the caretaker who could do no wrong. She was all those things, but in that moment, she was also vulnerable. She needed my help. I wasn't prepared for the gravity of the humanity of that situation, but I was so happy to be able to help.

What you need to understand about making money is that you should treat it as though it isn't all your own. My mother gave everything to me, and I felt so touched to have the opportunity to give back a fraction of what she'd given me. Giving filled my heart with joy, and I firmly believe it can have the same effect on anyone who wants to make the world a better place.

Without preaching to you, I want to share how tithing taught me about money. When I was growing up, my parents were adamant about giving 10 percent of the household income to the church. I didn't fully understand religion as a kid—all I knew was that we went to a Baptist church and that our pastor was a nice, retired military captain who spoke in a monotone voice. Frankly, I found listening to his sermons to be unbearably boring. I feel bad saying that because he was such a nice guy, but the man was not a natural orator.

Every Sunday when they sent around the offering plate, my parents eased my suffering a little bit by letting me put the check in the plate. I looked forward to this task so much because it was one way to get my mind off the maddening droning of the sermons. I loved handing over the offering, and I didn't realize until years later that my parents were training me to give money.

By the time I earned my own paycheck, the concept of giving money wasn't foreign to me, because I had practiced it a thousand times already. I'd given my parents' money in the past, but now it was my turn. Many people aren't used to giving money and struggle with it, but it's a practice worth working into your muscle memory. I'm not saying you need to give your money to a church, but invest some of your money into making the world a better place. There are people all around you who need help.

My favorite pastor talks about the quartet of the vulnerable: the foreigners, the immigrants, the widows, and the orphans. It's a list that has stuck with me as a reminder that there are always going to be people in need. Being open to helping those in need is one of the things that brings humanity into the world. People often want to help, but they don't want to know the story of the person in need. They roll down their car window and give a homeless guy five dollars because it's easy, but I think knowing people's stories is important—it's how you learn that you're a part of this bigger world.

Of course, there's a technical side to giving as well. When my brother pulled me aside to explain how my paycheck worked, he also told me that I needed to tithe, and I needed to tithe off of my gross pay, not the net. For sixteen-year-old Lorenzo, this was a tough pill to swallow. My paycheck was just shy of one-hundred dollars and he wanted me to take 10 percent off? But because Danny is my brother and board member, I knew he was coming from a good place. He was training me to not count on keeping all of my paycheck and to not spend money I didn't have.

Danny hit me with the reality that we have a responsibility to the world and can't just hoard all our wealth away. I struggle with this, but I'm so glad he made me give, because it forced me to look at my earnings and acknowledge all of the money isn't mine. If I can detach myself from some of that money, I can also give some of it to help other people who aren't as fortunate as me.

NEVER LEND MONEY

Another principle my parents taught me was to never lend money. My father often said, "The fastest way to lose a friend is to lend them money. If you're going to lend someone money, give it to them instead. Give it to them with no strings attached or don't give it at all, because they're never going to pay you back. You're going to get angry, you're going to hold a grudge, you're going to become bitter, and it's going to ruin your friendship. Give it away or don't give it at all." This principle has been one of the most profound principles of money I've ever learned and has even saved me friendships.

I was forced to deal with this principle sooner than I thought, which occurred during my teenage years at Gateway. The hundreds of dollars on my paycheck got a little bit higher and I started making some real money. I wasn't a salaried employee, but it was the first time I had enough money to buy some new clothes, eat at an Olive Garden, or spend it on a new cell phone.

At the time, a close relative of mine was in a lot of trouble. He was in and out of confrontations with the law and struggling to make ends meet. One day, he came to me and told me he was in trouble involving child support, a DUI, or fines of some sort. He needed to borrow six hundred dollars by the next day, or he was going to jail. As soon as the words left his mouth, my dad's voice started ringing in my ear. I saw his head over my shoulder saying, "Don't ever lend money. Either give it away or don't do it at all."

I looked at this close relative of mine and said, "Sure." Six hundred dollars was a massive amount of money for me at the time, and I'm pretty sure it cleared out my entire savings account, but I wasn't going to let my relative hang. I gave him the money, looked him in the eye, and told him,

"I'm giving this to you. I don't want it back." He protested and swore up and down that he'd pay me back, but I said, "Look, I know you want to pay me back and I appreciate it, but I want you to know that I am prepared to never see this money ever again." I'm so glad I said that because more than anything else, I was declaring to myself that I'd never see the money again.

Can you guess what happened? My relative ended up going to jail anyway, and the six hundred dollars didn't matter. He ended up not paying me back, but I still have a great relationship with him because I didn't go into the transaction with false expectations. I had released this person from responsibility by giving him the money, and I'm so glad I did. When you lend someone money, every time you see them, you think, "Hey, where's my money?" The other person starts avoiding you, and it creates a toxic environment that can kill relationships. For the sake of your friends and family, either give money away, or don't give it at all, that is, unless you want to get rid of someone.

The funny thing about that story is my relative never asked me for money ever again, which is saying a lot, because he had a reputation for borrowing money. He asked other relatives, but I never got asked again, and all it cost me was six hundred dollars.

THE THREE THINGS YOU CAN GIVE

There are three things you can give to make the world a better place: time, talent, and treasure. The beautiful thing about this trio is almost everyone can give at least one, but all three can have a great impact in their own way.

TIME

When it comes to giving time, the more skills and experience you have, the more valuable your time. The first time I ever met a tax accounting attorney, I was shocked to learn he made six hundred dollars an hour. I felt stressed every time I had to get on the phone with him, because I knew it'd be one of the most expensive phone calls I'd ever make. The price of the call was proportional to the value of his time.

When you have a skill, particularly one that's highly specialized, one of the best things you can give back is your time. Charities are usually happy to accept someone's time in lieu of money if that person can provide specific knowledge that they need. The chairman of the first charity I was associated with was an accountant. He gave back to this charity by helping them do their books and accounting, which must have saved them a ton of money, possibly more than he would've donated if he'd given money. In his case, it was better to receive a donation of his time.

Time donations don't need to involve specialized knowledge.

Doing something like ladling soup at a food bank, folding sheets at a hospital, or cleaning dog kennels at the pound are all valuable, necessary ways for you to donate your time.

TALENT

The second way you can give back is by sharing your talent. For example, when a charity needs a website or logo, they'll often try to find someone with true talent to come in and do the work for free. Frequently, someone will donate both time and talent at the same time. If you want to give back in this way, think about what talents you possess. Are you a talented builder? Can you perform music at a charity event? Talent can come from anywhere and from anyone.

TREASURE

Treasure is money, and of the three, it's the easiest way to give. For people like me who lack an abundance of time or talent, money is something you can share. As I get older, I realize my time is worth more, so I can donate it to people in the form of ideas and experience, but when I was starting out, the only thing I really had to give was money.

If you're not in a position to give money, you shouldn't feel bad. You can give in one of the other two ways. Don't feel bad if all you have is time and you don't have any money, or if all you have is money and you have no time. There's a reason there are three ways to give. Pick the one that works best for you and give back to the world in any way you can.

YOU CAN ONLY CONTROL YOUR ATTITUDE

—

"The key to humor is having an iron-clad sense of the absurd."

—BILL SCHLEY

The first time I saw people get what I would call unreasonably angry was during my job at Gateway. We sold computers throughout the year, but the closer we got to Christmas, the more we would tell people they needed to order by a certain date if they wanted to put their new computer under the Christmas tree.

No matter how well we communicated this concept, people ignored it and didn't get their packages in time for Christmas. Rather than recognize that it was their own fault for missing the deadline, customers became unreasonably angry. It was as if these people became possessed by demons. I remember a lady who came in one Christmas because she didn't get her webcam. Back then, Gateway was just a showroom, so we didn't actually carry any inventory. She demanded that we give her a webcam, but my manager tried to explain that the only thing we had were the display models.

She told him, "I am not leaving here without a webcam, even if I have to take that one right there."

His response was, "You can do that, but I will have to call the cops on you."

Of course, sometimes a real mistake would happen. The customer ordered a webcam, but the employee gave them speakers instead, for example. Rather than be understanding of human error, people lost their minds when mistakes happened. My first Christmas at Gateway, I went home feeling shocked by how poorly the customers treated people. I made a vow to never be that guy, and promised myself I would never treat a worker the way these people treated me and my coworkers.

During that same period, I was venting to my father about

awful customers when he dropped a bomb of wisdom on me. We were standing in the kitchen when he said, "Lench, the only thing you can control is your attitude. You can't control the customer, you can't control your boss, you can't control your other coworkers, and you can't control the weather outside. The only thing you can control is your attitude. Your attitude is a choice. You can choose to have a good attitude, but you will never be able to control any of those other things."

My father was absolutely right. There will always be angry customers in your life—that I can promise—but you can control your attitude. I made a decision that day to have a good attitude whenever I went to work. The decision paid off many months later in the form of a promotion.

My manager pulled me into a room one day and said, "Lorenzo, I want to tell you a story. Every morning, you come into my office to get the keys to open the store with a smile on your face, and you say, 'Let's get this party started.' Then you take the keys, and you go back onto the floor. Every morning you say that."

I had forgotten I said that because it had become such a habit. My manager said, "You have such a good attitude that I want to promote you, because it's things like that that really help the team get through their day." His compliment left me feeling so giddy, and I thought more about what he'd said.

"Let's get this party started" was my way of declaring I had a good attitude. It assured my team that we were going to have fun that day. Lastly, it was my way of holding myself accountable to the promise I made.

In the business of life, things will go wrong. There's no way to avoid it, but the way you prepare for bad things is by declaring that you're going to have a good attitude despite them. I'll admit that I've failed on this principle more than I've succeeded, but the times I've succeeded, times when I've lived this principle to the fullest, have been some of the best times in my work life. The times when I've chosen to ignore this principle were the most miserable periods of my life. Nobody's perfect, but don't let anybody convince you that they can control your attitude. You can say, right now, "I'm going be happy today. I'm going to have a smile on my face," and make it happen.

SHARING THE SPOTLIGHT

Giving someone a genuine compliment is a gift because it requires effort, and I've never seen such a spectacular display of this skill as when Graham addresses a crowd. When he's on stage giving a speech, he's the center of attention, but he'll look into the audience and see someone he knows. Then, he'll find a way to fit them into his speech and heap lavish praise and hearty approval upon them. I've watched someone grow ten feet tall sitting in their chair after Graham gave them this simple gift. In fact, it's happened to me.

When Julián Castro, the former mayor of San Antonio, stepped down to join the Obama administration as the secretary of housing and urban development, the city threw a big going-away luncheon for him. Graham was one of the keynote speakers at the event, which had several hundred people in attendance, including the whole city council and other San Antonio big shots. I attended along with a couple of my friends, like Dax and my pastor, Doug, and figured we'd hang around for a bit before leaving. In true fashion, I wore shorts and a "Keep SA Real" T-shirt.

In the middle of Graham's talk, he pointed at me and another colleague, Randy Smith, and said, "For those of you who don't know, Lorenzo runs my foundation and Geekdom, and he is one of my most important teammates. Randy runs Western Urban and is another one of my most important teammates. Lorenzo and Randy are really helping me in my efforts to change downtown."

I couldn't believe that Graham called us out in the middle of his talk to give us a compliment. I felt many things in that moment, most of all, terrified, embarrassed, and uplifted, because everyone in the audience turned around to look at me and Randy. It was one of those heavy, defining moments in life, after which people saw and treated me differently. People took me more seriously, and it was all because Graham went out of his way to call me out in a public forum. It changed the game.

BE LAVISH IN YOUR PRAISE AND HEARTY IN YOUR APPROBATION

One of the best books I've read on attitude is Dale Carnegie's *How to Win Friends and Influence People*. It's a book that changed how I interact with people and holds so many amazing lessons, but I'd like to summarize a couple of the best lessons for you.

The first lesson is to be "lavish in your praise and hearty in your approbation." In the spirit of full disclosure, I had to Google the definition of approbation the first time I read it. "Approbation" is a synonym for "approval." It means you should be generous when complimenting or approving of those around you. In practice, the lesson forces you to look for the good in people. I saw this practice brought to life to no greater degree than with Graham. Over the years, I've realized he's the defending heavyweight champion of being lavish in his praise and hearty in his approval.

In hundreds of meetings, I've watched Graham masterfully find real, authentic praise. Many people think lavish praise is flattery, but there's a difference between the two. Following the Dale Carnegie equation is difficult because it means genuinely looking into someone's life and character to find the good qualities. The quality could be something simple, like noticing how your coworker, John, always talks about helping his mother.

If you're going to stand on a stage and compliment someone in the audience, you need to really know that person to deliver a true compliment. It's not enough to put on a fake grin and call someone nice or say they look good that day. You can't fake it, nor should you try. Praise requires investigating someone as a human being and unearthing the gold within them. My advice is to make a habit of finding the good in people because it keeps you optimistic, makes the people around you happier, and acts as a force multiplier in your quest to have a good attitude.

A smile is another powerful instrument in your attitude toolbox. As Dale Carnegie wrote, "Actions speak louder than words, and a smile says, 'I like you. You make me happy. I am glad to see you.'" When I worked the check stand, you could always see which checkers had a million-dollar smile from all the way across the store. A customer would enter the store, walk to their line, and the checker would flash a big old smile that turned the customer to putty. I never had that gift, or never thought I had it, because I was too insecure to try, but smiling is one of the greatest tools in your attitude toolbox. It's a simple choice that tells people, "I'm happy to see you and want to help."

The trick is that your smile needs to come from a genuine place, because you can tell a real smile from a fake, not from the mouth, but from the eyes. Eyes give away the true authenticity of a smile, so think of something that makes you happy and let your eyes do the selling.

One final piece of wisdom from Andrew Carnegie is that most angry customers just want to be heard. When they're frustrated and upset, people want to feel like someone heard their complaint, understands their pain, and cares enough to help solve their problem. When I was a young account manager at Rackspace, customers' websites would occasionally go down, and they'd freak out. Out of necessity, I quickly realized that the customer was going to keep screaming at me until they were convinced I understood them.

I have a good friend and teammate, David Garcia, who has been serving customers longer than I have been alive. He told me his secret to deescalating a customer situation is what he calls, "The Three A's: Acknowledge, Align, Assure." The following example explains how it's used in the field.

When a colleague told me to call a customer whose site had gone down, I immediately deployed The Three A's. First, I'd investigate everything about their problem and take notes. Then, I'd call the customer, who was usually ready to explode at that point, and I'd walk them through step-by-step of what I understood about their problem. I would "acknowledge" what happened to them.

For example, I'd say, "Apparently at midnight last night, your website stopped working."

The customer would immediately jump in and say, "Yeah, that's exactly right. It went down at midnight."

"And according to what I know, nobody called you back until six hours later."

"That's exactly right. Nobody called me. I had to call in."

We would continue back and forth like this until they knew I understood their problem. It gave the customer a chance to vent their frustration, and it gave me the chance to convince them that their problem was now my problem and that I was going to fix it. This is where I would "align" myself with the customer. At the end of this process, the customer would usually be much calmer than when we started.

Your job with customers is to create a safe place for them to vent, because only after they've vented can you move on to the last A, which is to "assure" them that you will solve their problem. You need to convince them that their problem is your problem so they're on your side. Overcommunicate so they know you haven't forgotten about them. These are the tactics you need to successfully deal with angry customers. Keep in mind that nobody woke up in the morning wanting to call and complain about their service. They don't want to be dealing with their problem, so you need to let them vent by acknowledging it happened, let them feel hurt by aligning with them, and assure them you will solve their problem. Eventually, when you master the Three A's, you will turn a pissed-off customer into a friend. That is when the basketball hoop looks so big, you can't miss.

HOW TO PUT A GOOD ATTITUDE INTO PRACTICE

One of the most powerful phrases I've learned about attitude came from a coach of mine named Marney. Whenever I slipped and let my past dictate my future attitude, Marney would stop me in my tracks and say, "Would you rephrase that?" For example, I might say, "Oh, I'm just not good with discipline. I want to run so I don't have a heart attack by the time I'm thirty-eight, but I just can't because I never had any discipline growing up." Marney would stop me and tell me to try again. The correct way to reclaim my attitude is to say, "In the past, I haven't done a good job of running consistently, but today I've decided to get up early and run."

"Today I've decided" is a gift Marney gave to me that I'd like to now give to you. It's a phrase that can change the way you think, whether you're making a sweeping statement like, "Today I've decided to stop drinking," or a small, day-to-day choice like, "Today I've decided to have a good attitude." The choices you make today are under your control, and no one can make them for you.

You can put the past in its proper place—behind you—by deciding to do something right now. Focusing on the present and future is a tool a lot of people use to break addiction cycles like alcoholism. They'd say, "In the past, I drank too much, but right now I've decided to drink water." You have full control when you use "Today I've decided" to change your life.

Surrounding yourself with people who are going to encourage you and accept the fact that you've decided to change something today can help you succeed. If someone constantly reminds you of what you did yesterday, you need to fire them from your board and veto them from your life with extreme prejudice. Life is too short to fixate on the past, especially when you've made the decision to change today.

You want to find people who support you, but also people who see the absurdity in life, not the complainers. A good friend of mine and branding guru named Bill Schley says, **"The key to humor is having an ironclad sense of the absurd."** I think that saying is genius, because in the workplace, there's going to be absurdity. When websites went down at Rackspace, we'd occasionally get an angry customer calling to say, "You know how much money I'm losing right now? I'm losing a million dollars every minute. A million dollars! A million dollars every minute!"

When this happened, I'd perform a *30 Rock* Liz-Lemon eye roll. I still needed to solve their problem, but as soon as I hung up the phone, my team would joke about the absurdity of "I'm losing a million dollars every minute this website's down." The truth was that the customer was losing money, but they were using hyperbole to escalate their problem and create a sense of urgency. You can't call the customer out in this scenario and say, "No, you're not losing a million dollars, you dummy."

Your only recourse is to take that absurdity and turn it into humor. Humor is one of the most important ways to relieve stress in the workplace and bring teams together. I've always loved working with people who have an ironclad sense for the absurd—the people who make the day-to-day awesome. They make the world colorful, they make it hilarious, and they make horrible situations bearable. Having a good sense of humor is absolutely critical, but like a good attitude, it's a choice. When a customer yells at you, you can choose to find the humor and solve their problems, or you can choose to take it personally and hang up the phone feeling bitter and angry. Your attitude is your choice.

THE PERFECT MATCH TO A GOOD ATTITUDE: GOOD MANNERS

One of my parents' favorite phrases growing up was, "There's nothing worse than a kid with no manners." Throughout my life, I've realized that having good manners is an absolute superpower. I didn't realize it until I took a position where I worked on the phone. When you do support or sales on the phone, manners—or lack thereof—jump through the line and slap people in the face, because on the phone, all you have to work with are words.

Words provide one of the most direct ways to express manners. "Yes, sir. No, sir. Thank you, sir. Have a great day." These phrases are ways to show respect and were taken very seriously at my parents' home. If an adult asked me a question and I replied, "Yeah," my parents would lose their minds. If an adult asked me a question and I said, "Yes," my dad would nudge me in the back of the head and ask, "Yes, what?" He demanded that I answer "Yes, sir." The same applied if I ever got pulled over by a police officer. Pops said, "The only thing that should come out of your mouth is 'Yes, sir,' or 'No, sir.'"

Nobody told me until I was older how many doors good manners can open. I received one of the best compliments about manners of my life the first year I lived in London. I arrived in December and experienced a lonely Christmas by myself. I lived in an area just outside the city that was hard to reach, so everything in town was closed for the holidays.

A great friend of mine named Alexander Harris lived in London, but I had gotten to know him when he was visiting Texas. The first time I met him, we were smoking outside Rackspace in downtown San Antonio when he said, "I went to see your Alamo yesterday. Frankly, I have more history in my backyard."

I instantly fell in love with him. His parents lived in Oxford-shire in a house that was both older than America and appeared in every episode of *Downton Abbey*.

Alex called me on Christmas Day and said, "Mate, I'm sorry I can't be with you today, but will you come to my parents' house for Boxing Day?"

I said, "Of course," and Alex gave me some good advice on what to expect.

The next day, I wore my Sunday best and bought some flowers for his mother, then had the most nerve-wracking Boxing Day lunch of my entire life. I walked into the older-than-America house of this intelligent, sophisticated, British family. I could hardly contain my nerves, but my manners were on point. Everything out of my mouth was, "Yes, ma'am. No, ma'am. Yes, sir. No, sir. Thank you so much."

Alex's father was a pilot who'd flown for British Airways for years, and his entire family was well-read. Everything about them was so intimidating and the polar opposite of my universe. Before lunch, Alex had told me the rules of dining. There weren't many, but there was one very important rule, which was when you finished eating, you needed to set your knife and fork parallel to one another to signal that you were done with your meal. That was the most important rule I needed to remember.

I ate my food while my nervous brain said, "Don't smack your lips. Be engaging!"

Then, towards the end of the meal, Alex's father stopped and said, "Well, it's very apparent to me that Lorenzo was raised in a good home, because he has absolutely excellent manners."

I thanked him, but in my head, I was doing the greatest end-zone dance of my life. I was ecstatic!

If having good manners was the same as summiting a mountain, then I had just summited Everest. In my mind, the British invented manners and dominated the world market in being polite and gentlemanly. Having a British father compliment me on manners was like Albert Einstein telling me I was smart. I could do no wrong that day.

I was so excited to receive the compliment that I forgot to put my knife and fork together. Before I could undo all the good I'd done, I caught Alex's wife, Lucy, out of the corner of my eye making a little motion with her fingers, putting them together like a knife and fork. I quickly put my knife and fork together. She saved the day, and I wasn't reprimanded for my bad etiquette.

This event was one of the funniest things to ever happen to me, because I was a foreigner invited into someone else's home who didn't have to host me. At the very least, I could respect them by having good manners. I hope my etiquette said to Alex and his family, "This guy is worth having over again. He respects and appreciates what we're doing, and we will extend more courtesy to someone like that."

The question I have for you is this: Who in your life is going to extend courtesy to you? Who could you call right now to vouch for your good manners? If your manners haven't been so great in the past, that's okay—you can decide to change them today.

THE SINGLE, KEY COMPONENT TO A GOOD ATTITUDE

When you act with good manners, it sets you up to have a subservient attitude. Good manners show humility and thoughtfulness, and they communicate to people that you're not pretending to know everything. They demonstrate that you're willing to go out of your way to be respectful. Being respectful and subservient are, in essence, what makes a gentleman.

A gentleman has good manners because, when he pulls out a chair, he's serving you. He's putting himself in a lower social position, which is impossible for someone to do with a huge ego. Good manners and a good attitude affect all your interactions, and when you boil them down to a single, key component, you have humility.

Some of the best quotes on humility come from C.S. Lewis, the author best known for *The Chronicles of Narnia*. Lewis talks extensively about humility in one of his novels, *The Screwtape Letters*, which tells the tale of a senior devil writing to a junior devil about how to tempt humans. In the novel, Lewis describes humility in a unique way: "It's a state of mind in which he could design the best cathedral in the world, and know it to be the best, and rejoice in the fact, without being any more (or less) or otherwise glad at having done it than he would be if it had been done by another." I remember thinking that Lewis had created a new definition of what it means to be humble. It's about being as happy about the accomplishments of others as you are in your own. If possible, even happier. Humility is hard for people to achieve because it requires you to think of yourself less and think of others more.

In a book titled *Mere Christianity*, Lewis wrote: "Do not imagine that if you meet a really humble man he will be what most people call 'humble' nowadays. He will not be a sort of greasy, smarmy person, who is always telling you that, of course, he is nobody. Probably all you will think about him is that he seemed a cheerful, intelligent chap who took a real interest in what you said to him."

The paragon of humility in my life is my pastor, Doug Robins, and when I read that C.S. Lewis quote, I couldn't help but think of him. The first time I met Doug, I was going on a mission trip to Moldova, a country I knew almost nothing about. We were going to deliver jackets and shoes to kids in an orphanage as part of our giving back for the church. I remember it so well, because the name of the orphanage sounded so prison-like to me: Internat 2. I waited at the San Antonio airport security checkpoint with our church group, and I was pretty new, so most people didn't know me yet.

I had heard Doug preach several times before, so I had already developed a bit of a guy crush on him. I spotted Doug in the group and locked eyes with him. As soon as I realized he was looking back at me, I panicked, because I'm fairly antisocial and could tell what was about to happen next. Doug's eyes said, "I don't know this guy, but I need to know everything there is to know about him."

Like Gary Oldman in the *Dracula* movie, Doug floated over to me and was immediately like, "Hey, man, I'm Doug. Nice to meet you. What's your story?" Doug wanted to know everything about me, and it made me feel so special. Later, I noticed Doug was like this with everyone. It didn't matter if he crossed paths with a person with a face tattoo or a Mohawk; Doug needed to know about them because he was genuinely interested.

Genuine interest is the essence of humility. You can't fake it, but you can choose to take an interest in other people. After meeting Doug, I realized my approach to people was all wrong. I'd been treating people like a transaction: "Hello. I am me, you are you, let's get to business. What do you need from me, and what do I need from you?" Once humility enters the conversation, meeting people becomes so much more than a transaction; it becomes a relationship. I went from all business to: "Tell me everything there is to know about you. Oh, you have kids? What age? You love cats? I love cats, too. That's amazing."

Humility is choosing to look at the world through a different prism. It's not a virtue reserved for pastors and Mother Teresa; humility is something you can have, too. Above all, the combination of humility, humor, and a good attitude are the holy trifecta of superpowers you can claim for yourself today.

WHEN TO BE THE BOSS

"There is no utopia."

—POPS

Throughout your career, you'll notice that some people are never happy with their boss. I've found that when someone consistently thinks they could do a better job than their boss, it's time for them to be the boss. I don't mean you should stage a *Game of Thrones* coup d'état, but you need to become an entrepreneur and start your own company. So many people wait too long to become the entrepreneur they're meant to be.

Here's the problem: being an entrepreneur is risky. Your parents want you to go to school and get a job where you'll have safety and security, good health insurance, and a steady paycheck. All those things are questionable at best when you're an entrepreneur. But when entrepreneurs-at-heart are afraid to take the leap, they end up miserable and flailing around in their career because nobody told them, "You need to be an entrepreneur. You need to be the boss."

Now that I work in a coworking space around entrepreneurs, I finally see that some people are inherently suited to be their own boss. It takes a particular type of person, because being an entrepreneur is one of the hardest things you can do. Like having children or getting married, there's never a good time to do it, and it will never be easy.

My friend James Brehm is another fantastic sales guy I know, and throughout my career, I've seen him climb further and further up the corporate ladder. Finally, James became a partner at a boutique agency and started closing massive deals. One day, he looked around and realized that he was the one who provided most of the value at the agency. He thought, *Why wouldn't I just do this myself?*

James had the epiphany that he needed to be the boss, so he quit his job and started his own company. His company now works out of the Geekdom coworking space, is growing like crazy, and is bringing in a ton of revenue, and it's all because James realized that every step of the way, he saw ways companies could improve their processes. Not being able to change all the processes frustrated him, but nobody could solve his frustration except him. He was frustrated because it was time for him to be the boss.

James needed to create the world that he sought, which you can only do as an entrepreneur. So many people want to be the boss with the power to make their world as they see fit, while keeping all the safety and security that comes from a big company, but you can't have both. Entrepreneurship comes with a great deal of risk but also a lot of reward.

One of the cautionary tales people tell about becoming an entrepreneur is that your company is going to fail and that you're going to wind up destitute. I remember being on the phone with a woman who was leaving Rackspace after being there for ages. She had just had a baby, but I knew she was destined to be an entrepreneur. She called me because she was thinking about starting her own company, so I took the opportunity to encourage her.

I said, "Look, you need to go quit right now and become an entrepreneur. You haven't been happy with your last three bosses, and you're not going to be happy with the next boss. You're only going to be happy when you're the captain of your own ship. But here's the problem: you think you're going to quit your job at Rackspace and start your own company, then it's going to fail, and you're going to wind up homeless."

She started crying right there on the phone and said, "Yes, that's exactly what scares me. I'm going to be homeless, and I just had a baby—"

"Let me tell you something," I said. "I quit Rackspace and went to a startup called CityVoice. We went out of business. We fired everyone, including ourselves, and I am not homeless. You will find a way to figure it out. It sounds lame without specifics, but it's true."

That woman took the leap. She left Rackspace, started her own company, and she is ten times happier than I have ever seen her. Here's the thing: no one tells you about being an entrepreneur when you're growing up. The world says to find a job and suck it up. Sometimes that's the right thing to do, but **if you're never happy with your boss, you need to be the boss**. You need to quit right now and start your own company. Go into it knowing it will be extremely difficult and the odds are stacked against you. If you start a tech company, know that nine out of ten fail. Even with that in mind, you need to do it. You will never be happy in your current world, and more money won't fix your problem, because people who are never happy with the boss have an itch they need to scratch. So, ignore everyone who tells you not to do it, and do it.

CONCLUSION

WISDOM AND DISCERNMENT

"If in doubt, there is no doubt."

—POPS

Much of the advice in this book involves making decisions, so I'd like to share one final principle to help you navigate those choices. When we enter the workforce, we're told we need to do many things: we need to acquire knowledge, we need to learn, and we need to be good people. No one talks about another important part of maturing as an adult, perhaps because they believe it's hokey or spiritual—wisdom.

Wisdom is the missing component in the conversations we have in life and in our relationships. We rarely talk about wisdom, yet we see it all around us. When someone says a person has street smarts, they really mean the person is wise to the reality of the streets, that they understand the way the world works. It's a form of wisdom.

I want to take a moment to impress upon you the fact that I am not wise, and I don't want to convince you I am. I've made way more bad choices over the years than good ones. That said, the epiphany I've had in my life that I want to share with you is this: you need to start on a journey to seek wisdom. Wisdom is truly the pot of gold at the end of the rainbow. I wish someone had told me this sooner in life, and I want to save you some time. One of the great odysseys of your life is to seek and acquire wisdom and wise friends. You need to start that journey right now.

My dad had a saying when I was growing up that I didn't fully understand until I was older. Today, this phrase is one of my core beliefs: **If in doubt, there is no doubt**. This is the principle I want to give you as you make decisions in your life and career.

Growing up, I'd inevitably have a situation that called for this principle. I'd rehash details with my father and say, "My gut told me I should've done this, but I didn't, and the situation went sideways."

My dad would look at me and reply, "You know, if in doubt, there is no doubt."

It wasn't until many years later, when I read a book titled *Blink* by Malcolm Gladwell, that I saw this phrase of my father's broken down into its components.

The essence of *Blink* is that your brain processes data constantly. When you walk into a room, you're not consciously aware of it, but your brain has already picked up on the fact that the guy to your right has a frown, the lady to your left has a big smile, and someone in the background is doing jumping jacks. You might not notice all the small details of your environment, but your brain makes assumptions about the world based on that information. Its ultimate goal is to keep your happy ass alive.

In his book, Gladwell tells a story about a firefighter who enters a building after receiving a call. There's smoke coming out of some of the windows, but when he goes into the building, the room he's standing in has no fire. Immediately, he gets an instinctual gut feeling that something's wrong. The firefighter quickly says, "Everybody, out of the room!" As soon as everyone exits the room, the floor collapses. The fire was on the floor directly beneath them.

People interviewed the firefighter to try and figure out how he knew something was wrong. They discovered that this firefighter always walked into a fire with the earflaps on his helmet tucked up. He told them he did that to feel how hot a room was when he entered. On the day of the incident, he walked into the room and felt that the air was insanely hot, but there was no fire. He also told the interviewers that fires are very loud, but when he walked into the room that day, it was eerily quiet. Of course, we know now that the sound was muffled by the floor and the room was so hot because heat rises, but at the time, the firefighter's brain processed all that data and could tell something was wrong.

In the book, Gladwell calls this instantaneous data parsing and the ability of the brain to find patterns "thin-slicing." The firefighter's brain had thin-sliced the situation, connected the dots, and given his gut a bad feeling. Following your gut feeling is at the heart of my father's saying, "If in doubt, there is no doubt." If you have a bad feeling about a situation, something is probably wrong.

Sometimes, the right decision is obvious, and it's easy to make a call. For example, if someone on the street says, "Hey, stick this needle in your arm and you'll feel better," you know it's a bad decision. Other times, choices are more complicated and there's not a clear-cut, right-or-wrong answer. Those times are when you need to thin-slice the situation and follow the rule, "If in doubt, there is no doubt."

In my early high school years, I didn't have a car. I would either get my parents to drop me off at work or ask a friend with a car to pick me up. I had a good friend at the time named Ryan. He was a smart, blond-haired, blue-eyed guy with a great sense of humor who went to a tough, primarily Hispanic school in my neighborhood called Whittier.

One day, I got off work at H-E-B Number Five. I'll never forget what I wore that day: khaki Dickies, a forest-green H-E-B shirt, and a pair of Red Wing boots. Ryan called me to hang out, and we drove to Whittier. We went to the bleachers on the football field, which backed up to a neighborhood, and indulged our secret habit: Marlboro Light shorts. To this day, if I bring up the fact that I used to smoke, my mom will get up from wherever she is and come give me a light slap on the face and scold me about how smoking is terrible—but smoking's what we did that day.

It was about six o'clock, and the sun had begun to set as Ryan and I hung out on the bleachers because we had nothing else to do. The bleachers sat next to a twelve-foot fence that separated the school lot from the street. We smoked our cigarettes and chatted, probably about when we hoped Weezer would come to town, when a van pulled out of the neighborhood very slowly. This caught our attention, because most cars didn't drive that slowly in my neighborhood unless something bad was about to happen.

Ryan and I watched the van and nervously joked, "Ha-ha, drive-by." As soon as we said that, the doors of the van flew open, and five guys jumped out and ran towards the fence to jump it. Ryan and I instantly thought, *Oh, shit.* We leapt to our feet. This was the exact moment when, "If in doubt, there is no doubt" hit me in full force.

Ryan turned to flee, but I grabbed him by the arm and said, "Don't run." My gut told me that if we ran, we were toast. Ryan and I turned to face the five guys who had cleared the fence and were speed-walking toward us. Just like you see in the movies, the ringleader was the shortest of them all: a short Hispanic guy with a shaved head, wearing a white muscle shirt and carrying the bar from a dumbbell. Just the bar.

The ringleader strode forward and shouted a question at us: "Are you NBM?"

I didn't know what NBM was, but I could only assume it was the name of a gang. He asked us again and pushed the barbell into my chest.

All I could do was use what I had on me to my advantage. I replied, "Hey, man, we're not in NBM. Those guys are *putos*." I pointed to the H-E-B shirt I had on and told him I worked at the store down the road. I said, "My buddy and I were just getting ready to leave, and we're definitely not in NBM."

My gut told me something else: these guys were poor gangsters rolling around looking for trouble because they had nothing else going on. I reached into my pocket and offered the ringleader a cigarette.

The guy stopped in his tracks and said, "Yeah. Yeah, I want a cigarette." I said, "Cool, man. How about your buddies?"

I gave each of them a cigarette, and as I saw the temperature dropping in the situation, I said, "You know what? Why don't you take the pack? I'll get another one, because my buddy and I were just leaving anyway."

With a gift of cigarettes, I bought my way out of getting our asses kicked. The ringleader took the pack, and Ryan and I slowly descended the bleachers, then walked towards Ryan's truck while trying not to run. I figured that like I'd seen on the Discovery Channel, if you run away from the lion, it's going to chase you, and you're going to die. I didn't want to give those guys any hint that we were terrified, so we slowly walked to the car, got in, and left.

When people talk about street smarts, they're talking about having the instincts to handle situations like the one Ryan and I faced. My gut told me that if we ran, tried to fight the men, or did anything other than deescalate the situation with our words, we'd be dead. The guys came looking for a fight, but we gave them a gift that let them walk away from the situation still feeling like they'd taken something from us. No other event in my life embodied "If in doubt, there's no doubt" as much as that day it helped me survive.

YOUR HEART IS THE MOST MISLEADING ORGAN IN YOUR BODY

Pops always says, "**Your heart is the most misleading organ in your body.**" He's describing the difference between getting jumped by gang members and saying, "I'm going to fight them to uphold my honor," versus, "I'm going to run and try to get out of this situation alive." Raw emotions will mislead you.

For example, when you fall in love, you start losing all your objective, rational thoughts. You say and think crazy things like, "I'd swim the ocean for you." You can say whatever you want, but when you start making decisions based on pure emotion, you'll wind up in trouble. There's a place for emotion, but there's also a place for wisdom, knowledge, and counsel. If you don't believe Pops, take it from the famous French mathematician, Blaise Pascal, who once wrote, "The heart has reasons that reason cannot know."

Consider this classic romantic tale: two people meet in Vegas, drink until they're plastered, and then get married at the Elvis Chapel of Love. In the moment, those two people are probably going to chalk up their decision to romance, chemistry, or maybe even love at first sight. However, the heart is the most misleading organ. The chemicals that make you want to marry someone in Vegas are the same ones you get from injecting heroin; they're not exactly trustworthy. Don't make a huge, life-altering decision like getting married overnight because of feelings.

Particularly in a work setting, you need to battle emotion for more logical means of decision-making. You can either write the angry, pissed-off e-mail and hit "send," or you can save it as a draft and sleep on it. Only one of those reactions will help you advance in your career, and it's not the one ruled by emotion. My advice is to start building an arsenal of wisdom on top of knowledge, on top of counsel, and when your gut points you in a direction, trust it.

WHY YOU SHOULD SEEK WISDOM

As a child, I read the story of King Solomon right around the time Disney came out with the movie *Aladdin*. The concept of a genie coming out of a lamp and granting a wish was the most amazing thing in the world to me, and the story of King Solomon in the Old Testament was, to my young mind, the closest story in the Bible to the *Aladdin*'s genie.

Here's the short version of the story: One night, God appeared to King Solomon, the son of King David, in a dream and said, "Ask for whatever you want me to give you."

Solomon answered, "You have shown great kindness to David, my father, and having made me King in his place. Now, Lord God, let your promise to my father David be confirmed, for you have made me king over the people who are as numerous as the dust on the Earth. Give me wisdom and knowledge that I might lead this people, for who is able to govern this great people of yours?"

This story struck a chord with me as a child because God essentially says, "Because you didn't ask for money, fame, possessions, honor, or the death of your enemies, I'm going to give you these things anyway." Reading that story, I knew that I would fail the test. I grew up in the hood with a big family, so our money was stretched pretty thin. I probably would've asked God for a sports car or a pair of Red Wing boots, and I felt so ashamed when I read this story. I didn't think I'd be mature enough to ask for wisdom, like Solomon. I didn't understand what wisdom was at the time, but I knew I needed to pursue it.

The story of Solomon stood out to me for another reason; it was the first time I'd read a story of a leader who admitted he didn't have all the right answers. I'd grown up thinking the person in charge at least had to pretend to know everything, but here was a powerful man admitting he needed guidance. The pursuit of knowledge and wisdom should be commended, because no one has all the answers.

THE ROAD TO WISDOM IS PAVED WITH REBUKES

Proverbs says, "Do not rebuke mockers or they will hate you, but rebuke the wise and they will love you. Instruct the wise and they will be wiser, still." Most people don't like to get rebuked or corrected, and I didn't understand the proverb until the first time I was scolded by someone I admired outside of my family.

A man named Glenn Reinus, who is an absolute titan of industry, built the sales machines of two companies and took them public, then came to Rackspace to do the same. I'd look over at the sales team from where I sat and admire Glenn's leadership and the science he brought to the sales organization. One day, someone encouraged me to ask him for a mentor session, so I worked up the courage and invited him to lunch. To my surprise, Glenn agreed.

The day of our lunch, I felt so nervous. I took Glenn to a Fuddrucker's near our office and sat in the booth with a guy whose net worth I couldn't even comprehend. His experience was so vast that I was sure I could never ask all the right questions, but I tried. Glenn dropped bombs of knowledge on me and I soaked it all in. I told him, "Glenn, I'm so thankful. I appreciate it. Thank you so much. This has been amazing."

He waited until the end to scold me. As we wrapped up our conversation, Glenn looked at me and said, "Lorenzo, I want to give you some advice. The next time you ask someone for mentorship like this, have the courtesy to bring a pen and paper and write down some of these great ideas that you've heard today."

I wanted to crawl under the booth and never come out again. His suggestion was such a little rebuke, but it was so powerful. To this day, you'll never find me in a meeting without a pen and notebook taking notes. It turned out that a pen and paper is one of the greatest weapons of active listening you can have.

The act of sitting in a meeting and writing down what someone says changes the nature of that meeting. You send a clear message to the other person that you're listening and what they said is important. This was the wisdom that Glenn possessed, that I had not discovered yet, and he gave it to me in the form of a rebuke. I didn't love him at the time because I felt ashamed and embarrassed, but just like Proverbs said, I love him for it now.

Proverbs taught me wise people can accept feedback—they even seek it out. The question I have for you is, how do you handle rebukes? Are you receptive to them at all? Are you looking to improve in areas of your life? Having a personal board of directors is important because sometimes you can't take a rebuke from just anyone, but you can take it from your board. If you can't even handle rebukes from your board members, you need to work on becoming more open to criticism—it's the only way to improve.

WHAT IS WISDOM?

Wisdom is subjective and abstract, but one of my favorite theologians, Tim Keller, offers an excellent definition: "Wisdom is knowing the right decision to make in the vast majority of situations that the moral rules don't address."

This means there are going to be many decisions you have to make throughout your life for which there is no rulebook. YouTube, Google, and even your parents aren't going to have the answers. Wisdom is knowing the right thing to do, but there's no blog post titled "The Ten Steps of Wisdom You Can Implement in Your Life Right Now." A guidebook doesn't exist. However, there is plenty of literature that tells you, "These are the types of things wise people do," and you can learn by example. The examples wouldn't be as concrete as "Wise people wake up at six in the morning," but would describe characteristics and general practices. Wise people seek council. Wise people don't rush decisions. Wise people are patient.

Wisdom is a journey that most people don't know they're on. We were told as children to add knowledge, learn skills, and be a good person, but you'll seek wisdom for the rest of your life. It's a virtue we rarely discuss, but it is needed today more than ever.

THE DANGER OF EXPECTATIONS AND ASSUMPTIONS

Growing up, no one told me the world isn't binary, and that there are, in fact, many shades of gray. The primary difference between street smarts and book smarts is being able to see the murky in-between areas. With street smarts, you know there are some good guys on the street, some bad guys, and some people who are a bit of both. When someone approaches you on the street, street smarts tell you that you need to figure out what they *really* want.

Book smarts simply say, "Read this and answer that." It's good to have book smarts, but street smarts are equally important for life. There's no rulebook for the world, and if you're expecting one, you're going to be disappointed. Unfortunately, many parents don't teach their kids this concept, and it's certainly not taught at school.

I've seen a lot of people enter the workforce over the years with the expectation and assumption that the world is fair. They learn the hard way that there are backstabbers in the workplace, people will lie to your face and maneuver around you, and your coworkers will step over you to rise in their career. If you're not expecting these things to happen, you'll be devastated when your expectations and assumptions get shattered.

Mike Tyson once said, "Everybody's got a plan until they get punched in the mouth." It's one of my favorite quotes because it speaks to expectations and assumptions. When you expect and assume one thing, you'll have no backup plan when reality doesn't match. A similar phrase I've picked up throughout my career is, "There's the way you want the world to work, and then there's the way the world really works."

I see this problem with expectations and assumptions the most with startups. A startup founder will show me their plans and say, "We're going to create this website and put the button right here, and people will know to click it. We're going to get rich and become the next Facebook." Sorry, but no—that's the way they *want* the world to work. Then there's the way the world *actually* works.

Startup founders have an idea, but it needs to solve someone's problem to be successful. If it's not solving a problem, they have a gap between what they want the world to do with their company and what the world is actually going to do. No one is going to wake up and just go to their website for no reason. If their company isn't solving a problem, the world will ignore it.

If we look at the first assumption in the example, the founder assumed people would know to click the right button—not necessarily. The button might be the wrong color, have the wrong text, or be in the wrong place. There are people whose sole job it is to study user experiences and design websites for a reason. You need to be aware of the expectations and assumptions you hold for your workplace and work on learning the truth.

I've never seen someone use expectations and assumptions so effectively as a marketer. My boss Graham told me that Nick Longo, the cofounder of Geekdom, is one of the greatest intuitive marketers in the world. I didn't know what he meant until I started working with Nick and saw how attuned Nick was to the way the world really worked. Nick had created one of the first HTML editors on the Internet and had millions of downloads. He knew how to convert someone on a website, how to get them to click in a certain spot, and how to convey the right information.

One tactic Nick used was to tell the user where to click three times and to make the button extra flashy. Design snobs would say, "This layout is so cheesy and get-rich-quick," but Nick's designs worked. I'd watch Nick put together a website or marketing campaign and notice how he understood the way people think when they're shopping. At some point, something the customer saw on Nick's site made their brain switch from, "This is a good product," to "I'm going to buy this product," and it came down to Nick knowing how the Internet really worked.

The same principle of understanding your wants versus reality applies everywhere. Bosses want their employees to work one way, when they actually work differently. This divergence is why some bosses are total tyrants—the boss is out of touch with reality as to how employees really operate and doesn't know how to lead them. The tyrant boss ends up saying, "Just do what I want, because I'm the boss," without ever inspiring the team.

Wisdom is constantly trying to differentiate between the way you want something to work and the way it actually works. Take the time to identify your expectations and assumptions, and you'll be much more prepared to deal with the unexpected.

ACQUIRING DISCERNMENT AND ACQUIRING SKILLS

The equation to having discernment, which is the ability to make good judgments, is the sum of knowledge, experience, and counsel. Often, the people on your personal board of directors are the best source of counsel; they can help you find the real issues, coach you, and help you see issues clearly. Knowledge and experience, on the other hand, give you more data points. The more data points you have, the easier it is for you to make a decision.

My favorite podcast once explained that knowledge isn't enough. If you acquire skills, you can become a computer programmer. If you have knowledge, you can download an app on your phone. However, none of those things will help you determine if what you are reading on that phone is fake news or not. Only wisdom will guide you in making that judgment.

A long time ago, I took classes at a community college. One of my professors, a man named Steve Badrich, had us read Frederick Douglass's, *Narrative of the Life of Frederick Douglass: An American Slave*. The book profoundly changed how I view learning. It tells the story of how Frederick Douglass was born into slavery in the Deep South and became one of the most famous abolitionists later in his life. Douglass was so well-spoken that people didn't believe he'd been a slave. During his speeches, he would take off his shirt and show the audience the scars on his back from when he was whipped as a slave.

The story that really rocked my world described Frederick Douglass's life when he was young. He lived on a plantation owned by a man who wasn't necessarily mean but wasn't exactly nice, either. But the man's wife, Sophia Auld, was kind to Douglass. She taught him his ABC's and started teaching him how to read. One day, Sophia Auld's husband came in and flew into a rage when he saw his wife teaching Douglass. He said the best way to ruin a good slave was to teach him how to read.

Frederick Douglass, as a young child, saw this yelling match and understood. Wisdom told him that reading was a skill he needed to acquire. Why would learning how to read cause such a commotion if it weren't important? In the days after the fight, Frederick Douglass would take bread from the slave owner's house and go to the side of town where the poor white kids lived. He'd trade them the bread in exchange for reading lessons.

The quote that inspired me the most reads as follows: "When I was sent on errands, I always took my book with me, and by going about one part of my errand quickly, I found time to get a lesson before my return. I used to also carry bread with me, enough of which was always in the house and to which I was always welcome. For I was much better off in this regard than many of the poor white kids in our neighborhood. This bread I used to bestow upon the hungry little urchins who in return would give me the more valuable bread of knowledge."

Frederick Douglass, who was trapped in a prison of ignorance, knew that the only way to crawl out was to learn how to read. He taught me the true value of knowledge and turned learning into something tangible. He also inspired me to find innovative ways to learn.

When I took a typing class in high school, I panicked because I didn't know how to type. I would peck at the keys with one finger from each hand, but when my teacher saw me doing that, she covered my hands with a piece of paper. What I did next is something I'm admitting for the first time in this book: I cheated. I typed my lesson in a Word document and pasted it into the DOS program that we were graded on, and it shot my score up. I passed the class in this way, which is terrible.

Many years later when I was working at Gateway, I took the time to learn how to type in my own way. Because I knew typing well was important and I had avoided learning it earlier, I began covertly teaching myself how to type during the slow hours of my job. I learned about computers in general during my time at Gateway, too. A kind man named Jay, who was many years older than me, took apart a computer and explained everything inside in a way I understood. He said, "That's a hard drive, and it's like your closet. It's where you store all your files. This is your processor, and it's like the engine of your car."

It wasn't until my twenties that I began to enjoy learning and seeking out knowledge. Learning became fun because it was finally on my own terms, and I was usually able to read something and immediately apply it to my job. A friend of mine named Ajay Rayasam shared a story with me that furthered my appreciation for knowledge. Ajay had a mentor named Jim Lewandowski, who was a successful executive. One day, he told Ajay, "You shouldn't be worried about what you're going to make money-wise this year or next year, or even in five years. You need to worry about what you're going to make in ten years, and the only way to affect that is through skills acquisition."

Skills acquisition is critical to your career and personal growth. I had learned a few skills at H-E-B in produce and a few more at Gateway, but it wasn't until I worked at Rackspace that I was able to feast from the buffet of skills. I didn't realize it, but I was acquiring MBA-level skills for free. The chance to learn and acquire skills is something I took advantage of, and I want to encourage you to seek the same opportunities.

THE FEAR OF LOOKING STUPID

One of the most powerful forces in the world that can hold you back from achieving your goals is the fear of looking stupid. When I went to Gateway, I realized I knew nothing about computers and it scared me. I was afraid of looking like the guy from the hood who didn't know anything about the world.

Growing up, I had a computer my uncle gave me that I could never get to work. One time, I got it to turn on and used its word processor. Between the word processor and my high school typing class, that was about the extent of my computer experience. However, I recognized that computers were important and would only become more important in the future. I knew I had to learn about them.

The first thing I did when I started at Gateway was to follow my advice from a previous chapter; I assumed the apprentice role. I didn't try to fake my knowledge when I got to Gateway—I couldn't. Faking it would've been obvious in a second, so I told people I had no idea what any of the equipment was, but I'd ask questions.

People like it when you ask questions because it tells them they have valuable knowledge, so my coworkers were happy to help me. I was open to learning new skills and forced myself to be vulnerable about my lack of knowledge—I had to overcome the fear of looking stupid. For any really dumb questions, I knew I could count on my board members to answer without making fun of me. With their support, I began learning new skills.

COWORKERS

Your coworkers are often the best resource for you to acquire new skills. At Rackspace, I was friends with two engineers named Jay Bridges and Tim Bujnoch. Something the engineers did that I considered pure wizardry was logging into servers, and one day, they showed me how to do it. They showed me how to install Terminal Services, add an IP address, and type in the admin credentials.

Suddenly, I knew how to log into a server, and I thought I'd become a hacker. The point I want to make is good coworkers like Jay and Tim will invest time in you so you can acquire new skills. Everyone benefits when this happens. Jay and Tim didn't need to explain as much to me, and as a result, I could explain servers better to our customers. They weren't trying to make me an engineer; they were trying to give me some skills to help me be a better account manager and a better colleague.

In your world, think about which of your coworkers can teach you new skills. When you think of someone, you need to ask them. People don't always offer to help, even if they're willing. Most of the time, people want to show you how good they are at their job. You'll have coworkers who are curmudgeons and resistant, but you'll also have coworkers who are intuitive teachers—they're the ones you want to find.

LEARN BY DOING

On-the-job training is another excellent way to acquire new skills. At H-E-B, I learned how to cull produce by identifying fruits and vegetables that were going bad. The difference between book learning versus on-the-job training is the difference between reading that a tomato darkens as it spoils versus grabbing a tomato you think is ripe and having your hand go through it. Knowing what a rotten tomato looks like versus feeling it. If you have no good coworkers to learn from, where in your world can you learn things hands-on?

In my later years at Rackspace, the company offered me two directorships that came with fancy titles and big pay raises. The offer was a big deal because I was only twenty-eight at the time, and in order to be a director, the board had to approve the promotion. Two of the executives at Rackspace approached me. One said, "Lorenzo, I want you to be a director of project management. We're going to work on these challenging, exciting projects. Some of them have stalled, but I think you can pull them off."

The other executive said, "Lorenzo, you're the kind of guy people love working around. We want to create a new position that focuses on the culture of Rackspace, and we want you to be the first one to take the role." I had a real dilemma on my hands. That night, I went home and stared in the mirror, then asked myself, "How am I going to make this decision?" Then I recalled my friend's advice that Jim Lewandowski had given him.

Which of the two jobs would allow me to acquire more skills? The culture position sounded fun and exciting, but it also fit the bill of "looks like work but isn't." I didn't know what skills the role would help me acquire. Also, I had a gut feeling that if the company started doing badly, the culture role would be one of the first to go. I looked at the director of project management role and thought, *There's a job where I can get some real skills.*

I took the project management job, and it was one of the

best decisions of my life. I learned about taxonomy, Six Sigma, Gantt charts, and all kinds of other tools and skills that would help me advance my career. Everything I learned, I still use to this day.

A lot of people try to get away from difficult work, which usually means getting away from the customers. I will say it again: staying close to the customers is essential for job security. Along with that, people want easy jobs, but you should find one that challenges you and gives you the chance to learn new skills. There are always more skills to learn, so don't take the job that lets you coast by on what you already know.

MY READING DISCOVERY

My parents have always been avid readers, but growing up, I only ever read comic books. My outlook on reading could not have been more off. I thought the main purpose of reading books was to memorize just enough to pass a test at school and not have my parents be angry at me for failing. I didn't discover that reading books was actually a thing that people did socially until my twenties when I lived in London. I hung out with a group of three guys who read constantly and always referenced books in conversation. After spending some time with them, I started to develop a queasy feeling in my gut that said, "Oh, shit. You don't read books, dude. This is a red flag."

I worried my friends would ask me about the books they read and I wouldn't know anything—I'd look stupid. Or worse, they would see I wasn't adding anything stimulating to the conversation and drop me as a friend. When there's a real intellectual deficit between two people, the relationship can become intimidating for the person who's less well-read. One of the guys, Ben Frewin, solved the problem for me when he gifted me with a copy of *Freakonomics*. I thought, *This is my chance!* I could make up for my lack of reading and join their conversations. I took the book home and absolutely devoured it.

After that first book, I went crazy with reading. My Norwegian friend Jon Andersson and I would talk about Hemingway and Kilimanjaro and running with the bulls, and it all stemmed from immersing ourselves in a culture of reading. Everyone needs to read. Starting can be as simple as picking up a *Marvel* comic book. It doesn't matter how you start, as long as you open a gateway to other books.

Pick up a book that interests you. Sometimes, you just want to read good stories. Other times, you want to read business books. I often get business-book fatigue, but when that happens, I turn to the classics. I pick up Hemingway, *The Iliad*, or Robert Louis Stevenson. There are books out there better than any Netflix series; you only need to find them.

I've had friends and family members recommend books

that I found terrible and other books that never let me down. My pastor, Doug Robins, is one of the people whose suggestions never disappoint. For some reason, Doug has recommended more business books to me than anyone else in my career—and he runs a church. It goes to show you that anyone can read anything for any reason. I love learning about the things I'm involved in every day, while other people love reading about things entirely new to them. Both are completely valid choices.

As I got older and read more, I learned a principle: when I was young, I didn't know that I didn't know anything. The more you read, the more access to information you have and the more you realize how much there is to know in the world. Now, I know that I don't know anything, and I can do something to fix it. As an adult, the great thing about reading is no one can make you do it. When you're in school, you're required to read and adhere to a class deadline. When I was a kid, this approach soured me to reading for a long time, mostly because I was a slow reader and still am. When you're older, reading is your choice. No one can mandate if, when, or what you read, but believe me when I say reading is one of the great pleasures of life and you shouldn't deprive yourself of it.

Aside from being enjoyable and allowing me to participate in well-read conversation, I discovered that reading made me better equipped to sell my ideas. Books gave me data, which is what makes or breaks an argument. I could tap into brilliant minds, borrow ideas, test them out, and use them to sell myself and my ideas. I realized, with the world's information at my fingertips unlike any other generation in human history, there's no end to what I could learn.

THE GREATEST COMPLIMENT I EVER RECEIVED

When I started at Rackspace, Graham Weston was already a local legend—smart, knowledgeable, successful, and yet still down-to-earth. I'd seen him in company meetings and said hello to him in the hallways, but I had hardly spoken to him before. One day, I was on the support floor when someone announced that Graham didn't want to be in an office anymore. He wanted to be in the middle of the action.

The coworker turned to me and said, "Lorenzo, you have the only open cube, so you're going to share it with Graham." This was the moment I panicked and realized I had no idea what I was doing. I felt sure Graham would hear me talking to customers on the phone, realize I knew nothing, and have security walk me out of the building—but that's not what happened.

Graham sat next to me, and we instantly connected. I admired him, but I couldn't understand why a guy of his knowledge and background would want to get to know me or be interested in what I had to say. Nonetheless, we developed a relationship over the years where I'd tell Graham my thoughts.

About once a year, I'd walk into his office and say, "Graham, let me tell you something. That manager over there—you should fire him because he doesn't care about customers. But this other guy is amazing and you should promote him."

Graham would raise his eyebrows and ask, "Really? Who else?"

I'd reply, "Well, let me tell you who else is terrible." I'd talk on and on, and in retrospect, I was so dumb and ignorant about the way of the world.

I didn't realize what a special, truly remarkable person Graham was, but I also didn't realize I was establishing credibility with him every time I walked in his office. I was building trust because I wouldn't say, "You know, Graham, I'd be an amazing manager!" I'd go in and say, "This is our company, and this guy's messing it up, and you need to take care of it." Then I'd leave and get back to work.

When I went to London, Graham would call me and ask me to give him the real story on things that were happening. Again, I'd say, "Well, let me tell you what's going on." We developed an amazing rapport. It wasn't until I worked directly for Graham—the person I shared a cubicle with and had barged in on over the years to talk about rotten employees—that I realized he was from another universe and that I didn't belong anywhere near him.

You see, Graham comes from a family of successful entrepreneurs and innovators. When I started working for him, he'd been the executive producer of a documentary called *Lord Montagu*, which is about a famous uncle of his. We flew to London for the film's premiere, and I remember thinking, "Here we go. This is going to be another boring documentary about a rich white guy." In reality, the documentary blew my mind.

The film talked about Graham's mother, Caroline Weston, whose maiden name was Caroline Montagu of the house of Montagu in England. Graham's mother grew up in a royal estate called Beaulieu in the New Forest of England. The original patriarch of the family bought the estate from the King of England and was the king's lawyer.

The family was the patron of William Shakespeare, who was rumored to have done two of his first plays at Beaulieu Estate, where Graham's mother grew up. Graham's mother's father, Lord Montagu, was in the House of Parliament and was one of the first people in England to pioneer the automobile. He believed automobiles were the future, even though the rest of the aristocrats of the time ridiculed what they called "horseless carriages."

Lord Montagu was the Elon Musk of his time—an advocate of new technology. He was so involved in promoting new technology that he commissioned the hood ornament for his friends—Rolls and Royce. That is to say, the hood ornament of the Rolls-Royce was commissioned by Graham's grandfather as a gift. Lord Montagu went to Parliament and told them they needed a system called license plates to register all the vehicles. The man was truly remarkable.

Lord Montagu died, and his young son, the new Lord Montagu, Graham's uncle, inherited his estate. This happened right after World War II when Britain's economy was in shambles. Anybody who owned a huge estate couldn't afford to maintain it because the city would tax you based on how many windows you had. Many of Britain's lavish homes, like *Downton Abbey*, were burned by their owners and rebuilt smaller so the family could afford it.

Lord Montagu was a talented entrepreneur, and I started to realize where Graham got his gift. Montagu was the first lord to open his house to the public. He decided to let the everyday people see how they lived to make a bit of money. The aristocracy absolutely hated him for it, but Lord Montagu was an entrepreneur. He was able to generate money to maintain the estate that had been in his family for centuries.

The other aristocrats, being under the same pressure, started opening their houses. Montagu, being an innovator like his father, said, "I will differentiate." He placed his father's first car and several other automobiles in the living room of his estate. All of a sudden, Beaulieu Estate became *the* place to see motor vehicles. The attraction was so successful, Montagu raised money and opened the National Motor Museum of Britain on this estate.

My friend and mentor, Graham Weston, spent his summers as a child at this historic estate. I couldn't believe how a down-to-earth guy who grew up on a ranch in Marion, Texas, could be related to so many accomplished individuals. Graham's father's side of the family was equally impressive. Garfield Weston, the great patriarch of the family, had started a cookie and bread empire in Canada and Britain, and owned some of the greatest grocery chains and bakeries in those countries.

I learned Graham had this deep heritage of technology, entrepreneurship, and innovation, and I realized how unworthy I was of his friendship, which is why I want to end this book with a story of the greatest compliment I've ever received.

Just before I started working directly for Graham, I left Rackspace to go to a marketing startup called CityVoice. I joined the company at the tail end of their funding and worked a nine-month sprint. Even though we hit our revenue goals, churn goals, and had more potential inventors wanting to give us money, my gut told me something was off. One day, the CEO, my dear friend Matt Schatz, and I were outside smoking a cigarette when he said exactly what I was thinking, "I don't think this business is going to make it."

We fired everybody at CityVoice, including ourselves, and it was the worst day of my career. As I began to look for a new job, the chairman of CityVoice told me about a big project in downtown San Antonio and said I fit the demographic they wanted. He invited me to come learn more about the project at a charette. A couple things went through my head at this point. First, I thought, *I'm a young Hispanic guy who's out of work. Surely, you don't want my demographic.*

My second thought was, *What the hell is a charette?* I pulled up Google and discovered *charette* is a fancy word for a brainstorming session. I figured I'd go to the meeting for a bit and eat a few French pastries with names like "charette," but I didn't expect much else to come from it. I went and learned about the big plans people had for the city I'd grown up in, but by the time lunch came around, I was ready to leave. As I stood to go, Graham walked in and shook everyone's hands. I told him I was taking off, but before I left, he suggested we catch up.

We met about a week later at one of Graham's favorite places, Marie Callender's, and sat at a booth in the back corner. We caught up a bit, and then I told him, "Graham, don't be mad. I need to go back to work, but I realize that I'm a hippy and can't work for a big corporation like Rackspace anymore. I need to go somewhere small where I can make a difference." I braced myself and told him I was going to go work for a competitor of Rackspace's called Peer 1 Hosting.

Graham was not happy. It was the first time he was ever upset with me. He pulled out his iPad and showed me how Peer 1's financials weren't great and how the company wasn't growing like Rackspace.

I argued that I didn't care about those things and told him, "My best friend Dax works there, and I want to go work with someone I enjoy being around. I want to make a difference again."

When he realized I wasn't making a rational decision, Graham said, "Don't work for them. Work for me."

Then the tables turned, and it was my turn to get upset. I told Graham I knew how people treated him, and I refused to be one of them. People always asked him for money and favors, but I didn't need anything from him. I was not meeting with him for a handout or a job.

Graham gave me a fatherly grin and did a little Jedi mind trick as he said, "Let me tell you something, Lorenzo. I know that as soon as this other company pays you a dollar, you're going to give them 100 percent of your effort and loyalty. I want to pay you the same dollar and get 100 percent of your loyalty and efforts for me, instead."

His words stopped me in my tracks. I called Dax and told him about my talk with Graham. Dax, being one of the great board members of my life, told me I had to take Graham's offer. It was a once-in-a-lifetime deal, and he said if I didn't take it, he would never talk to me again. I accepted the job, went to work for Graham, and discovered he's a passionate philanthropist. He had a plan to revitalize all of downtown San Antonio and kickstart a tech scene from the ground up, but I had no idea he wanted me to be a part of it.

Graham's office at Rackspace was a tiny room with white-board walls, a giant wall-mounted monitor, laptop hookups, and piles of markers. It was the perfect space for Graham because he's an idea engine—a great entrepreneur like his family members. I'd meet with him every month to go over current and potential projects. We'd debate and I'd ask questions. Every once in a while, he'd say, "You need to read this book, Lorenzo. It changed my career."

One day, Graham and I were debating a radical idea, and I thought I went in too hard. I pulled back and said, "Graham, I'm sorry. I just got very passionate. I didn't mean to come off that forceful."

Graham looked me dead in the eye and said, "Lorenzo,

because you read and constantly seek knowledge, I always want to hear what you have to say. Always."

It was the greatest compliment of my entire career. J.R.R. Tolkien said, "The praise of the praiseworthy is above all rewards," and Tim Keller once paraphrased it by saying, "We all want someone we think the world of to think the world of us." The day Graham told me I belonged in that room was the day I realized I had the praise of the praiseworthy.

There I was, a young Hispanic guy from the hood with no college degree and no credentials, sitting in a room with a man who has a family legacy of success and innovation. I told Graham what I was feeling, but he was quick to reply, "You belong here. You have the credentials, and the credentials are that you seek knowledge, you read, and for all of these reasons, I value your opinion."

So many times in my career, I have looked around and thought, *No one in my neighborhood will believe what I'm doing right now.* I've seen things that no one from my neighborhood has probably ever seen. I've met people no one from my neighborhood will probably ever meet. All of that was made possible because of other people, not me. I have been a traveler on a fantastic journey because of the kindness of others and because they saw potential in me that I didn't see in myself.

It is my hope you will go out and have your own amazing journey. I hope you learn from my faults and double down on the hard-fought insights. I hope your board is full of love and warmth. I hope your mentors take you to places you have never imagined. If you don't have support, it's okay. I hope you'll let this book be another mentor or even your first mentor. I hope it will be a board member to you when there is no one to give you advice.

My mentor Doug Robins once explained to me that a group of rhinos is called a "crash" because rhinos can run up to thirty miles per hour but can only see about thirty feet ahead of them. A personal board has this kind of power. Most people have bought into the lie that only the lone wolf achieves a great career. I am here to tell you that both life and work are a team sport, and like the rhino, you become a force of nature when you do it together.

So my challenge to you is this: Go pick up another book and read it. Go share your ideas with a mentor. Go find a board member and deputize their ass. And just like the rhino, go pick up so much steam that your posse comes crashing down onto your future success. Only then can you claim your rightful place in the winners' circle and hang your picture above the cilantro at H-E-B Number Five.

ACKNOWLEDGMENTS

I have worked on this book for over a decade with no success. It was not until I found Book in a Box that I found new hope that I could bring it to life. Without their team, this book would not exist. First, thank you, Dan Bernitt, for being the first person outside my friends and family who saw potential in my story and said yes. That decision changed everything. If it can be said that there is an architect to a book, that person would be Barbara Boyd. She is the "Defender of the reader" and took all the thoughts floating around in my head and brought order and direction. If writing a book is like climbing a mountain, then there is no doubt that Lauren Holstein is my Sherpa. I would not have summited without her constant encouragement and patience.

I would like to thank Kara Gomez for her love, support, and for her council that always happens to be right.

I want to thank David Heard for introducing me to Book in a Box. Khaled Saffouri, who not only helped me pitch my book and was on the first phone call with me, never stopped encouraging me to keep going.

I want to thank my personal board members who read drafts or excerpts of the book and for their genuine feedback. They are Dax Moreno, Pravesh Mistry, Luke Owen, Doug Robins, Randy Smith, Emily Bowe, Alexandra Frey, Carlos Maestas, Jake Gracia, DJ Gracia, Steve Cunningham, and Danny Gomez Jr.

I want to thank the bona fide authors who read and lent their experience to me, which was worth its weight in gold. They are Bill Schley, Bob Rivard, and Laurie Leiker.

Thank you to Cruz Ortiz for designing a cover that makes me smile every single time I look at it. It captured the essence and style of my stories in one picture.

Lastly, thank you, Graham Weston, for believing in me all these years. You have treated me like a son and opened doors that would have never been available to me. You changed my life.

ABOUT THE AUTHOR

LORENZO GOMEZ III began working in customer service as a teenager, more eager to earn experience than a paycheck. As a produce clerk in a grocery store, he realized job satisfaction was more than having his picture displayed above the cilantro bin. Driven to advance his work life with little college experience, Lorenzo utilized valuable lessons from his entry-level jobs to catapult him into high-impact positions. Having gained insight throughout his career journey, he advises young adults that fulfilling work and career advancement come from learning from others, understanding how business really works, and knowing how to thrive in any work environment.

Serving as CEO of Geekdom, the largest coworking space in Texas, and as cofounder of the 80/20 Foundation, a philanthropic organization, he puts best practices to use, collaborating with a diverse network of professionals to fortify growth of a tech district in downtown San Antonio—an ecosystem he helped create. As a tenacious team player and technologist with a passion for entrepreneurship, Lorenzo is paying it forward by sharing his on-the-job experiences so that young adults can learn and understand how complex business principles can be observed and applied in the most unlikely places.

His professional experience stems from Rackspace, the largest managed cloud provider, where he worked closely with Graham Weston, cofounder. Lorenzo is a cofounder of Tech Bloc, and he serves as board member, advisory board member, and mentor for a variety of local and national tech and entrepreneurial organizations.

Made in the USA
San Bernardino, CA
26 March 2018